A
Journey
Into
Dreamland

A Journey into Dreamland

What it's like there, why we go there, how we get there.

A dream is the mental equivalent of a warp in the fabric of spacetime.

John P. Rogowski

E-BookTime, LLC
Montgomery, Alabama

A Journey into Dreamland

A Journey into Dreamland is the revised, expanded and improved version of *Properties of Dreams: A New Theory of Dreaming* published in 2011. The expansion is in the form of its final chapter, *The Twin Photon Theory of Dreaming*, the result of our rapidly increasing knowledge of quantum physics.

ISBN: 978-1-60862-677-9

First Edition
Published June 2017
E-BookTime, LLC
6598 Pumpkin Road
Montgomery, AL 36108
www.e-booktime.com

To
My parents
and
teachers

all are gone but not forgotten.

ILLUSTRATIONS

PREFACE

I don't remember my first dream or my last or any in between except the one that is documented in Chapter 5 to illustrate the construction of dreams. Most were remembered briefly, never more than a day or so, but all are gone now. I am only able to recall three insignificant snippets of dreams widely separated between the ages of twenty and eighty, the sole products of spending over five and a half years of my life dreaming. That's not much to show for that investment of time and superb creativity.

I don't know how old I was when I began to understand what "dream" meant. I vaguely recall that it was at a very early age that my mother would comfort me in the middle of the night, reassuring me that a scary night excursion was "only a dream". It has been a long journey (about eighty years) from my understanding of the word, dream, to the *Twin Photon Theory of Dreaming*. It required intense study of dreams as omens, as predictors of the future, as problem solvers, as useless residuals of the day's mental activities, as guardians of sleep, as royal roads to and from the unconscious, as the hidden complexes of Freud and as bodyguards for REM (rapid eye movement) sleepers. In my case the journey was needlessly prolonged by the twenty year Freud stopover which was wasted on the obsessional decoding of cryptic symbols. It took that amount of time to cure myself of the singular obsession with the *what* of dreams, and direct my attention to their *why* and *how*. The *what* of an object under scientific investigation is answered simply by observation; in dreams it is the dream content (simple enough). The *why* is the reason it exists; in dreams we want to know in what way the dreamer benefits from the product of his creativity – not an easy task to find out but doable. The *how* has to do with construction. We want to know how the dreamer is able to perform his amazing feat of dreaming without even trying. To find out is a formidable task that requires the reductionist approach used in quantum physics.

It makes no difference what we know about dreams, gravity or the many other laws that govern us, our knowledge cannot change them. No one is above these laws. They have good reasons for being and must be rigidly enforced – no exceptions, zero tolerance.

I frequently wonder why I got into this messy preoccupation with dreams. It could be because dreams are messy, and we seem to have a need to create order out of disorder. But the problem with dreams is that they MUST remain disordered; that's part of the dream law. How can such disorder have purpose, and what is the purpose? Better yet, what are the purposes? I never learned in school or through mentors how to construct dreams out of subatomic particles, yet I do it four or five times a night. How do I do it? How do you do it? The task herein is to answer such questions.

Choosing an ontological/teleological pathway, inspired by Copernicus, has, for me, been productive of important insights about dreams and nature in general. I believe these insights are worth sharing with the world wide community of interested dreamers.

In this book I have avoided all footnotes because in my reading I have always found them distracting. The contents of the putative footnotes have been inserted into the text. The glossary is extensive because several sciences are involved, the terminology of which all readers may not be familiar.

Because of the similarity between the written and spoken words "proton" and "photon", and since they are both used in the context of sub-atomic particles, one must be careful of misreading one for the other.

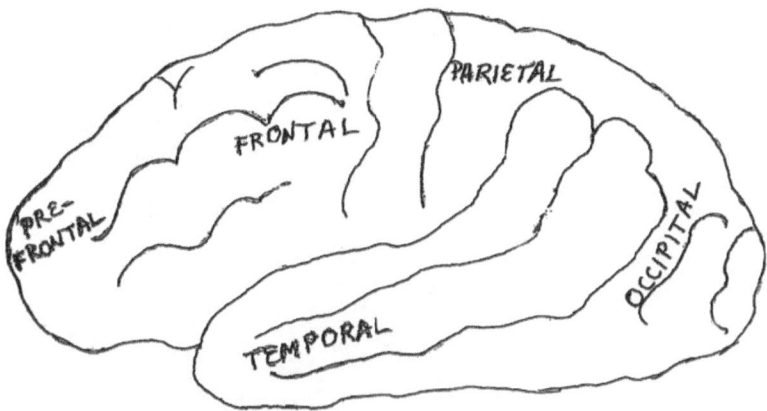

Figure P The left side of the brain with its five lobes. For the sake of simplicity and for our purpose, consider the main functions of the pre-frontal and the frontal lobes to be thinking, executive functions, short term memory and movement, of the parietal lobes to be perception, of the temporal lobes to be long term memory and of the occipital lobes to be vision.

INTRODUCTION

All of the 7.2 billion dreamers, who inhabit this planet, awakened at one time or another, amazed, puzzled, entertained or scared by a dream experience. Many have wondered about the how and why of dreaming. Some have embarked on careers to formally investigate and explain the phenomenon. None have been successful.

Where others have failed, the author makes the effort by suggesting a novel pathway that includes evolution, relativity and quantum physics. He claims he has the credentials for such an undertaking because he is a retired psychiatrist who has listened to hundreds of dreams in his many years of clinical psychiatric practice, is an amateur astronomer (indicating a scientific bent) and a professional insomniac, who no longer resists his sleeplessness, but labors nightly from 1 to 5 A.M., as he has for dozens of years, in his personal dream lab. He now properly considers dream science his career. Admittedly, it does seem strange that a non-sleeper should regard himself an expert in dreaming; actually, he does sleep and dream before and after his four hour shift. He claims that just as gravity has its laws, so does dreaming, and he knows them and is willing and eager share them. The experiments that he urges the reader to perform are simple and only require an eyeball and a finger. The reading is

1

effortless and enjoyable, even for those who are unversed in the mysteries of non-classical physics.

Science doesn't have to be complicated. Einstein once claimed that "it should be possible to explain the laws of physics to a barmaid". This book is best described as popular level science, which means that it can be understood by high school graduates who have had the usually smattering of the sciences, and may or may not have continued their formal scientific education. Such individuals are not scientists, but may be highly motivated to expand and extend their knowledge of science, in this case, dream science.

Since Freud's *Interpretation of Dreams* many new observations of the phenomenon have been reported in scientific journals, the most important of which have to do with REM (rapid eye movement) sleep and what happens in the brain during dreaming. Old and new theories as well, of how nature works, are, as a matter of fact, useless junk. Our knowledge or lack thereof does not change anything; the Sun rises as it didn't prior to the heliocentrism of Copernicus, we still fall off ladders the same as we did before Newton's inverse square, energy still equals mass times the speed of light squared, as it did since the beginning of time, long before Einstein quantified the explosion, we still dream as we did prior to Freud's symbols and Aserinsky's REM sleep, and it will remain so no matter what new theories arrive on the scene. There is no crucial demand for new theories of anything (except in the case of doctoral candidates whose livelihood may depend on a theory proposing something new and different). In spite of the fact that new theories change nothing, consuming and digesting them *somehow makes the brain, like the stomach, feel good.* A new theory of dreaming is offered because we have grown tired of the stale Freudian dream menu, its symbols, its censor, its latent and manifest dream content. It fails the prevailing appetite for modern dream science with its neurotransmitters, mitochondria, brain imaging and open mindedness; it no longer makes the brain feel good. Even though the bookshelves remain loaded with Freudian pseudo-science in the form of tempting symbol dictionaries, dream encyclopedias, dramatic psychoanalytic case histories, psychological mystery novels and even romances, scientific minded readers ignore them. Freud has found his place in the fiction section of bookstores and libraries, a most undignified place for any scientist. May he rest in peace there.

Although Aserinsky (1921-1998), Dement, Kleitman, Jouvet, Hobson and many others, who are now engaged in the dream research industry, have made significant contributions over the past half century to the physiology of dreaming with their discoveries related to REM sleep, they appear to be currently mired in neurophysiology when they should be moving on in the direction of reductionism that only physics can provide. *A Journey into Dreamland* does not ignore but builds on their discoveries and introduces a new theory, vastly superior to Freud's because it is bona fidedly scientific and more complete than that offered by experimental neurophysiology.

Focusing on the why and how of dreams and their utilities, the author supplies simple and understandable, visual illustrations and experiments to help the readers in their comprehension of the basics of relativity and quantum mechanics, as they are intertwined and entangled with dreaming.

He makes good on his claims that: all dreams MUST be crazy, or we would be in big trouble if they weren't and dreams are difficult or impossible to remember because it is NOT important to remember them. Once they have done their job they become as useless as last week's supermarket shopping list. Dream content is not important – the *act* of dreaming is. Furthermore, he boldly states, ***"A Dream is the mental equivalent of a warp in the fabric of spacetime."*** This simple definition, which explains so much about dreams, is so powerful that one can almost hear all that dream stuff click in the brain.

It makes sense that the laboratory of the mind should be the most fitting place to investigate mental phenomena, in this case, the investigation of dreams. Everyone has access to such a lab. While working there on whatever project, one should keep an open mind, and frequently remind one's self of this quotation from Copernicus (1473-1543), which will be repeated in whole or in part, several times when appropriate,

"... we should follow the wisdom of nature which as it takes very great care not to have produced anything superfluous or useless, often prefers to endow one thing with many effects."

It will help the reader to understand my thought processes and the route I intend to take. It not only states that everything that is is useful, but that what is, frequently, has more than one use. Our goal is to discover the primary usefulness of dreams, a very arduous task, and their much less arduous secondary and tertiary utilities.

Why do we want to take on such a task? It makes no difference in our lives if we succeed or fail in determining the primary utilities of dreams or anything else. They will continue to be unchanged by our knowledge or lack thereof; they are meant to remain unchanged; they are governed by immutable laws. This also holds true for the secondary utilities. The tertiaries, on the other hand, are the products of man's creativity, and as such, we are in control of them; we can change them and manipulate them to our advantage. Man uses properties of objects with primary and secondary utilities to construct the tertiaries of those objects. It is we who have made a place for tertiaries in our lives whether to facilitate our survival or to make our lives more comfortable and pleasant. The survival benefits of the tertiaries differ from those of the primaries and secondaries in that they benefit only select segments of the population. Any utility that shows evidence of man's creativity is designated as tertiary.

When it comes to dreams, as with anything that is mental, there are relatively fewer and less impressive tertiary utilities that we can identify because they can't be physically manipulated the way we are able to manipulate material object. Nevertheless, with considerable difficulty, I have been able to come up with the following tertiaries for dreams: as a source of income, thereby enhancing the lifestyle of dream analysts, instructors in lucid dreaming, fortune tellers, psychics, omenists and other predictors of future events and, yes, authors of dream books (like me). Fortunately, there are people who read such books for their intellectual enjoyment and to satisfy their curiosity to know how and why things work. Obviously you are one of them. We are rewarded with an immense feeling of satisfaction from finding out. The more evasive the how and why, the greater is the satisfaction in their discoveries.

Having listened to hundreds of dreams, because that's what psychiatrists do or did, I have concluded that all dreams are essentially the same; they follow the same laws – we all dream the same way. That being so, I have decided to focus on my own dreams, not especially on content but on why they are, how they came to be and what would happen if they weren't. My goal was to extract understanding from what, in the beginning, seemed beyond understanding. Not having the training of a researcher or experimentalist, I felt at a great disadvantage and loaded with self-doubt.

Eventually, I came to the realization that the raw material was there aplenty and that I had a rent free dream lab that was open for business all day and a good part of the night. (Non-dream sleep is the only time that the lab is not open.) At night I would passively collect the data through my dreams, and during the day, remembering them, I would make the effort, when time allowed, to understand them and form some reasonable, if imperfect, explanations for my dream experiences.

Thought experiments, as performed by Einstein, Bohr, Heisenberg, Schrodinger and others to solve extremely difficult problems of quantum physics, were not limited by matter and consequently, required no material measuring tools. It is likely that many of the great scientific discoveries were the result of thought experiments which were later validated by experimentalists in material laboratories. In spite of the fact that I had no access to a material sleep lab or an electroencephalograph (EEG) machine, I realized that I had everything that I needed to investigate the phenomenon of dreaming. There were the dreams themselves, which I experienced firsthand rather than through hearsay (as I had done as a psychiatrist), there were memories of the memories, that is, I was not only able to remember some dreams but also was able to make connections to the memories used in the construction of those dreams, and, of course, there was that portable laboratory of my mind where I was able to do my thought experiments any time, any place.

Periodically, in my investigation of dreaming, I experienced overwhelming joy as the great science theorists must have experienced with their monumental discoveries. Unfortunately, with me, more frequently than not, the joy was followed by heart breaking disappointments resulting from theoretical flaws exposed by further dream experiences or the interpretation of them. It is not a good feeling to wake up in the morning to discover that you have scribbled several pages of junk the night before; the discovery being the result of a dream that demanded that your theory be discarded or modified. But, after all, isn't that what experimental laboratories are for – to challenge theories and in challenging successfully, to discard or modify?

Einstein, allegedly, has been quoted as saying, "If the facts don't fit the theory, change the facts." Surprised and disbelieving at first, upon further thought, I realized that he was entitled to such arrogance since he did just that, as did Copernicus, Kepler, Galileo and Newton. Keep in mind the "facts" of the fifteenth century were no longer the facts of the twentieth century and the "facts" of the twentieth century (I have in mind Freud and Darwin) should be properly challenged in the twenty-first century. However, those who, like me, are deprived of the intellectual gifts of Copernicus, Kepler, Galileo, Newton and Einstein will do best in making our theories fit the "facts" of the centuries we live in.

Not knowing how or why things work does not prevent them from doing what they do. When Copernicus proved heliocentricity, although it was the discovery of the millennium, it was irrelevant to the life of the ordinary individual; night still followed the day, winter became spring, then summer, then fall. Belief that the Earth was the center of the solar system or that the Sun was the center made no difference. Eventually however, that discovery did make a difference for the common man. It led to the invention of a reliable calendar, the discovery of the laws of gravitation and the space age with its jobs, jobs, jobs. What I am saying is that even the greatest discoveries have no immediate practical applications but place investigators on a track of experimentation, further discovery and inventiveness, all leading to a benefit for mankind. James Clerk Maxwell (1831-1879) or was it Michael Faraday (1791-1867), (historians disagree), both pioneers in the discovery of electricity, was confronted by some smart aleck politician, "So what is electricity good for?" His response, after a brief moment of thoughtfulness was, "Well maybe the queen (Victoria) can tax it." Now that's what one would call a creative tertiary utility.

In my opinion, we have been on the wrong track with Freudian dream theory for seventy years, and a new theory of dreams and their utilities is long overdue. Although of little consequence today, hopefully it will put dream investigators on a novel path, eventually leading to new treatments for psychosis, being that dreams and psychosis have so much in common. Consider the time, effort and money that could be saved by the abandonment of ineffective treatments, springing from flawed dream theories.

How does one go about in determining the utility of dreams? We begin by admitting, as Copernicus did, that all things have one or more reasons for being even though, at certain points in time, they may be hidden from the observer. Here and now in 2016 A.D., because of our ignorance of the mind/body relationship, we are unable to build machines that would allow us to prove experimentally our theories of mental functioning. Currently, we have to be satisfied with the brain itself and its ability to reason, interpret, introspect and reflect on itself and its functions; we have to be satisfied with its ability to create theories in such a way that one can almost hear things click into place and its ability to correct, by logic, errors that come from within it. Do we need a better instrument? Einstein arrived at many of his creative ideas not by laboratory experiments but by his thought experiments; his laboratory was in his mind.

In Chapter 12 (Light) we perform several experiments suggesting that the eyeball itself, when deformed, is capable of releasing light. This is easily proven in the first experiment and is reproducible from subject to subject. The second experiment in which we attempt to make a connection between the eyeball deformation in REM sleep and the light production that occurs in visual dreams lacks the reproducibility of the first from individual to individual and even in the same individual, because of yet undiscovered variables.

None of these experiments are in the same category as Galileo's acceleration of falling bodies, Newton's light refraction experimentum cruces or Einstein's curvature of the fabric of spacetime, all of which can be viewed by outside observers. The light production by deformation of the eyeballs can only be viewed by the individual performing the experiment;

it cannot be shared with others. It can only be demonstrated to one's self; it is limited to the confines of the experimenter's brain. It cannot be photographed, but it can be drawn, as the author attempts to do in Chapter 12. These drawings are presented so that they may be compared to the observations of the reader.

A Journey into Dreamland is divided into three parts with some mixing in and overlapping, an unavoidable but desirable connectivity. The first part (Chapters 1-5) deals with the "what" of dreams: the dream content (the primary interest of Freudian dream psychology), the common knowledge of dreams that all dreams are crazy, that they are difficult or impossible to remember and that they are constructed by the interaction of creativity with memories. The second part (Chapters 6-11) deals with the "why", the utilities of dreams, primary, secondary and tertiary. The third part (Chapters 12-13), the "how" is derived from the close scrutiny of the author's own dream experiences and experiments, leading to a theory yet to be confirmed, modified or discarded by readers, amateur and professional. I feel that the theory is complete, but admit to holes that are yet to be plugged up. I welcome additions, subtractions and corrections of the errors that inevitably slip through the cracks.

All of us have viewed a falling body, and for the great majority of us it ends with the view. For certain individuals, in this case Galileo (1564-1642), seeing was not enough; he gave such events close scrutiny, speculated uniform accelerations of falling bodies, set up an experiment with an inclined board and water clock to prove it, and wrote his famous equation. This is the universal road for the discovery of physical laws, i.e., close observation followed by speculation and verification by experimentation. Unfortunately, mental phenomena, such as dreaming, are resistant to physical experimentation because of the mind/brain barrier. They remain mostly but not completely in the realm of speculation.

PART ONE

WHAT IT'S LIKE THERE

Chapter 1

COPERNICAN CLUES

*"...we should rather follow the wisdom of nature,
which as it takes very good care not to have produced
anything superfluous or useless..."*

N. Copernicus

The usefulness of most things that we encounter in life become immediately apparent. Dreams are an exception; they do not have utilities that are easily recognized. When questioned about the utility of dreams, my colleagues find it difficult to come up with satisfactory answers. Disenchanted with Freudian dream analysis over the years, they have lost interest in dreams as diagnostic and therapeutic tools of their profession, although they are still interested in the personal experience of dreaming. In the second half of the twentieth century, patients expected their psychiatrist's office to be furnished with a couch and anticipated and eagerly awaited the request to tell their dreams. Times have changed; now it is, "Don't ask, don't tell". And if a psychiatrist wants to avoid civil or criminal suits for sexual misconduct he should forgo a couch and settle for a desk and two chairs and well, maybe a picture of Freud on the wall.

Many mental health professionals now claim that dreams are simply the waste products of the day's mental activity, that they have no meaning and are useless. They are unimpressed when reminded that urine, which is the waste product of physical activity, is an invaluable medical tool that allows us to diagnose over twenty pathological conditions and with time, may be useful in over a hundred.

Other utilities of urine include: returning nitrogen to the soil, claiming one's territory (mammals other than man) and what every good Boy Scout knows, its usefulness in extinguishing the too slowly dying embers of a campfire. It is also useful in the competitive game that little boys play of "who can pee the farthest" (girls not included because they are poorly equipped for this game, sorry).

Three clues that confirm the Copernican counsel include:

- universality
- automatic rhythmicity
- time investment.

Dreaming appears to be a universal phenomenon. But there may be people out there who do not dream. In fact, I have run across quite a few patients who make that claim. However, on more careful questioning, they concede that what they really meant was that they didn't remember their dreams. There was another group of "non-dreamers" who feared that their dreams were so crazy, that if they admitted to them, they would be committed to a mental institution on the spot. It is important to keep in mind that: ALL dreams are crazy, and if they were not, we would be in deep trouble, and dreams are difficult to remember because it is NOT important to remember them. These are two not so surprising claims, (give it a little thought, and you will agree), and they will be elaborated in later chapters.

It is difficult to imagine that anything that is universal, either physical or mental, could be useless. On the other hand, how can something as crazy as a dream, even though it is universal, be useful? No wonder that even professionals throw up their arms in resignation and claim that dreams are the useless waste products of mental activity.

The claim that dreaming is universal is appropriate even though I admit to the possibility of exceptions. Just as the human genome demands us to have four complete and nicely functional limbs, there are some people born with only two, either because a rogue cosmic ray collided with that special gene in Mom's egg or because she used Thalidomide to get a good night's sleep during her pregnancy. The universality argument should be sufficient to convince those skeptics who claim that dreams are the waste products of mental activity, that dreams must have some utility and it must be important. Dreaming among humans is so universal that in the course of evolution, it seems logical, that only the ones of us who learned how to dream have survived; the others perished on the path to Homo sapienship.

For those that are unconvinced, I offer another clue: We dream automatically. It happens without us giving it any thought. We cannot make ourselves dream or prevent ourselves from dreaming. We can fairly compare dreaming to the automaticity of respiration and the beating heart. Nature gives us many choices in life, to dream or not to dream is not one of them. When there are no choices, it usually means that whatever we are not free to choose is part of our genetic makeup. I believe this is true of dreams; dreaming is in our genes. The centers for the automaticity of breathing and heart beating are in the lower brain stem (the medulla oblongata). There is some evidence that the center that controls the automaticity of dreaming is in the middle brain stem (the pons).

The rhythmicity of respiration and heart rate is variable depending on the needs of the body. Breathing and heart rate increase with exercise, and decrease with inactivity. The rhythmicity of dreams is variable depending on the needs of the mind. Dreams occur four or five times during the course of eight hours of sleep. The duration of each dream increases gradually as the time of waking approaches. Normally, the *number* of dreams we have is directly proportional to the amount of sleep we get, strongly suggesting that if dreams have some utility then that utility is only available during sleep. Insomniacs need not be concerned because they don't need dreams when they are awake – dreams do nothing for us when we are awake. Well, maybe they entertain us after the fact. Moreover, if, for any reason, e.g., insomnia, attending to the needs of a sick child or being unable to close a book, we lose sleep and dream time, when we finally do fall asleep there is a tendency to make up for the lost dream time by further expanding the *duration* of dreaming, another indication of the importance of dreaming when sleeping.

A more dramatic example of the need for a certain amount of dream time is offered by J. Alan Hobson, psychiatrist, talented dream experimentalist and researcher and prolific science writer. He theorizes that delirium tremens (DTs), a syndrome caused by alcohol withdrawal manifested by delusions, illusions, visual hallucinations and amnesia occurs as the result of a decrease in REM sleep associated with prolonged use of alcohol. When alcohol is withdrawn a rebound effect occurs whereby REM sleep is increased to such an extent that there is a spillover of dream craziness into the waking state. Since many illnesses, including psychoses, which are associated with symptoms of delirium, are preceded by sleep deprivation and, consequently, a decrease in REM sleep, we should be looking for the same kind of rebounding described by Hobson.

Over the average lifespan, the time invested in work (U.S.A. 35 hours/ week) is almost eight years, in dreamless sleep it is about nineteen years, for dream sleep it is about five and a half years (about one-sixteenth of your life). Can you imagine Mother Nature, who has laid down strict laws for the conservation of matter, energy and momentum, allowing her favorite children to engage in the useless pursuit of dreaming? It would seem in her wisdom she would eliminate dreaming and pull the plug of our life support five and a half years sooner. Logic tells us that something we experience but not necessarily remember four or five times a night from toddlerhood to old age and saps our conscious and unconscious energy must, in some way, be useful to us and not in a trivial way. The question is: Why would we need five and a half years of the useless activity of dreaming (a total of about ten thousand dreams)? Can't it be diminished by a little bit? It is estimated that there are one hundred billion stars in our Milky Way galaxy, and there are hundreds of billions of galaxies in the universe many of which have far more stars. In a few years, with much more powerful telescopes, the number of stars in our universe will be estimated in googles (google $=1\times10^{100}$). One wonders if all those stars and dreams are necessary or is God just showing off. What would happen if one itty bitty star or dream was subtracted? Laplace says the future would be changed.

Pierre Simon Laplace (1749-1827), a mathematician and astronomer of the genius type, was also known as "The French Newton". He wrote five volumes on celestial mechanics, and in what is known as "Laplace's Demon", he expounded on causal determinism with the claim that if an intellect existed that knew the position and momentum of all the atoms in the universe, that intellect could predict the future in the smallest detail. Corollary to this would be that if just one atom was subtracted, the future would be changed significantly or insignificantly but changed. This supports the Copernican view that nothing is superfluous or useless – not a single star, not a single dream.

Some would argue that having the plug pulled five and a half years sooner would be a pragmatic solution to the economic problems facing this nation since it would allow massive cuts in Social Security and Medicare spending, less taxes and a more enjoyable life style. Given a choice, I would prefer the dreams and happily bear the burden of more taxes.

Just as the neurotransmitters demolished Mr. Censor and, consequently, Freudian dream theory, I believe that universality, automatic rhythmicity, time investment and the words of wisdom of N. Copernicus have demolished the useless "Waste Products Theory of Mental Activity". So where does that leave us as far as a theory of dreaming is concerned? It leaves us with dreams as omens or predictors of future events, which, since you have the intelligence to read this book, you have immediately discarded – no further discussion necessary.

Dreams, now in a theoretical vacuum, are begging for their usefulness to be recognized. We offer a new theory of dreaming – very new and very compatible with the scientific advances we have been fortunate enough to witness in the past century.

Chapter 2

FUN WITH FREUD
(1856 - 1939)

"A cigar is just a cigar"
S. Freud

In September 1952, when I was barely twenty-one, I met him for the first time while browsing through the stacks in the library at Georgetown Medical. He didn't belong there! What was he doing there? There were rumors, but he didn't look like a pervert (they seldom do). Pictured in sepia, he resembled a professorial aristocrat: elderly, bespectacled, bearded, cigared, tweed suited and wearing a large gemstone ring. I met him from time to time after that but only at a distance and by accident, and when that happened, from the back of my mind there always emerged those damnable, damning rumors fueled by his *Theory of Infantile Sexuality.*

Four years later, after I completed my degree, our paths seemed to cross more and more frequently and less and less by accident in places where intellectuals and pseudos tended to gather, libraries, bookstores and bars. The seduction started with his fascinating tales of dreams or rather the interpretation of them, his fears and his wishes. He made all kinds of promises about our future together. How could I resist? I fell in love. In spite of the differences in our ages and faiths and the lack of difference in our genders, we were married. Freud was the answer to all of my dreams. My colleagues scoffed.

As the years passed, I became uncomfortably then painfully aware of his warts. We separated after twenty years of intellectual fidelity; we are now amicably divorced. (Breaking up was hard to do; I gave Sigy the best years of my life.) As happens in many failing marriages, that which had been the main attractive force becomes repulsion; her lilting laughter becomes a cackle, and his witty conversation becomes as entertaining as the obituary page. In this marriage, as you might have suspected, it was the interpretation of dreams. (Of course, my brief affairs with Aserinsky, Dement, Kleitman, Jouvet, Hobson and others did not help.) To this day, I have the greatest respect for the man; in fact, that magnetic personality continues to adorn my refrigerator door, reminding me of the good times as well as the bad. Although I still yearn for the passion of those youthful years, I know I could never live with his dreams again. It is painful for me to talk about, yet, I know I must.

I was infected, as were millions, by the contagion of his dreams which spread bubonic-like or more happily, Beatle-like over Europe and the United States. One can understand such an exponential increase in interest since dreams are entertaining, miraculous, mysterious, fantastic, humorous, romantic, educational, crazy and scary. Like television, dreams are entertaining, but they can become somewhat annoying because of the frequent and capricious changing of channels. Even nightmares can be entertaining (that is, after the fact), and I have asked my wife not to awaken me during a screamer in which some faceless, malevolent monster is chasing lead legged me off a thousand foot cliff in the middle of Long Island Sound.

The entertainment value of dreams cannot justify their universality, automatic rhythmicity and time investment. These properties are indicators of some very important functions that may, at times, be as necessary for survival and sanity as breathing and eating are to life.

Upon awakening, most people struggle to make sense of their dreams which, I believe, attracts many to the analyst's couch. They have been educated to believe that understanding their dreams will make good on Freud's promise to cure them of their "complexes", allowing them to live more happily ever after.

Freud made two important observations about dreams: that they were the "royal road" to the unconscious and that they were the guardians of sleep. In this context the unconscious refers to the pervasive unconscious *mind* rather than the unconscious state which occurs with head trauma, anesthesia or dreamless sleep. The unconscious mind is simultaneously accompanied by awareness of one's existence. Freud claimed that what was happening in the unconscious could be revealed through the interpretation of dreams. "The royal road to the unconscious" implies a one way street. I believe the royal road is a two way street; in one direction dreams lead to the contents of the unconscious mind, while in the opposite direction the contents of the unconscious mind, e.g. repressed and suppressed memories, lead us to dreams.

Fatigue and its attendant chemical changes are the guardians of sleep. In addition, I am in agreement with Freud's observation that dreams also have such a guardian function. In dreams we are observers but with markedly more intense involvement than we experience when watching a movie drama. We become *participant* observers. We want to stay in the dream theater; we don't want to leave even though it may be scary to stay. The drama is complicated, which adds to our determination to stay and figure out the plot. Somehow, we know that if we awaken the show is over. Who would want to leave and miss all of that fascinating nighttime entertainment?

A movie begins with, say, a roaring lion, the title of the movie and a list of characters. From the beginning and throughout the performance we know that we are non-participating observers. The plot evolves gradually from the beginning to middle to end, which, if properly written, allows us to leave the theater with a sense of satisfaction, like having enjoyed a nice meal. How different is a dream. It is as if we dropped down from out of nowhere into the middle of an ongoing event, and whether we like it or not, we become participants. We don't seem to know the beginning; we don't know where we were before we got there; we don't know how we got there, we just appeared there. And we don't even know why we're there, and we don't care. Then, after a while, as if the projector suddenly broke, the show is over; there is no more dream.

Critics, who are in the know, would rate all dreams as negative four stars (-****) because the plots are invariably written sloppily and incoherently. Seeing that kind of movie is not only frustrating but also useless, a waste of time – yet we seem to be addicted to it; we keep going back for more. We can do without such crazy night-time entertainment or can we?

To make things even more complicated, Freud claimed that what we dream is not what we really dream. (Such infidelity to common sense keeps popping up in Freudian psychology.) He claimed that the manifest dream content (what we are aware of as the dream) is really a secret encoded version of the latent (hidden) dream content. The encoding is done by the symbolic representation of objects, actions and conflicts. The dreamer, by himself, is unable to decode the dream and is unable to find out the latent dream content. Freud said that we should be grateful to nature for that because the contents of our latent dreams are so evil, so repulsive, so scary, so ego dystonic, so loaded with broken taboos that it would do some sort of immeasurable damage to our well-being if we found out. Mother Nature is so good to us.

Now if there is such a code loaded with symbols, there must be an entity that does the encoding. Freud realized that, and so he invented and included in his theory of dreams the "censor", best imagined as an anthropomorphic being that Mother Nature hired to protect us from all that evil stuff that lurks in the unconscious mind of man. His job is of the utmost importance – without him Freud's theory is doomed to collapse.

(It is odd that avowed atheist, Freud, who flaunted his atheism, could not find compelling evidence for the existence of God because, like many other scientists, he could not measure, weigh or time Him, yet he found no problem in inventing and believing in Mr. Censor who was also unmeasurable, unweighable and untimeable.)

For being a censor, he behaves in a most peculiar way. When government agencies want to maintain secrets that may be embedded in certain documents their censors simply redact those parts that might leak a secret. What is peculiar is that Mr. Dream Censor doesn't redact but takes the trouble to present us with an encoded version of those horrible secrets. It seems that he doesn't want us to know, yet he does want us to know. He is teasing us. One would think that the dream censor would simply redact the entire latent dream content and thereby, make manifest dreams useless and unnecessary – no more dreams.

(Animal lovers frequently attribute human traits to their pets. One wonders if animals dream, as many pet owners claim. And do they also have both manifest and latent dream content with a dream censor that protects them from finding out their nasty unconscious secrets, or are latent dreams with their censors a late evolutionary arrival reserved for man alone.)

Freud was aware of the dilemma: the risky business of knowing those latent secrets and the horrible fate that such knowledge holds in store for us versus keeping them hidden, thereby allowing them to sap our mental energy in the preservation of secrecy. Freud solved the problem by training individuals, mainly psychiatrists, in the science and art of dream analysis. They would be the official decoders of dreams, trained to be aware that great care must be taken to do it *gradually* or some horrible fate might ensue. That's why psychoanalysis must be protracted over years, (also because time is money).

Dream analysis is, at best, a fantasy and, at worst, a fraud. Do we really believe that there are latent dreams accompanied by their constant protective companions, the censors? It appears to me that there is more science in astrology than in dream analysis.

Psychoanalysts are extensively trained, and they themselves must be analyzed by a training analyst. Of course, Freud, as the founder of psychoanalysis, was psychoanalyzed by himself because there were no trained analysts that preceded him. He himself could not reap the benefits of his own creativity. He had to be his own analyst and analysand at the same time or else live with his unresolved complexes. Poor Sigmund!

Complexes are unconscious conflicts that exist in Freud's putative latent dreams. The conflicts are between our uncivilized animal instincts (the id) and our civilized self (the ego) and are not pretty. The most popularized conflict is the unacceptable desire for an incestuous relationship with one's mother, known as the Oedipus complex. YUCK!

Freud, who had no special interest in the why and how of dreams came up with a dandy, profitable tertiary utility by concentrating on the interpretation of the dreams of the well-heeled curious, somewhat similar to the interpretation of astrological signs so popular in the past with royalty. That is the creativity of a genius.

The following is a fictional account of a dream as a Freudian analyst would dissect it. (If Freud is entitled to introduce fiction with his latent dreams and censors, hey, so am I.)

Thomas is a mathematics professor at a prestigious university. Now in his forties he is bored with his job and, more importantly, with himself and his stale thoughts. Never having come up with anything as elegant as Einstein's energy equation, Newton's inverse square or the Pythagorean Theorem, he felt intellectually constipated. He frequently was afflicted with anxiety bordering on panic and "psychosomatic" ailments, the most excruciatingly painful of which was peptic ulcer. Seeking the meaning of existence, he had taken up the solitary avocation of astronomy and built an eighteen inch Dobsonian, grinding and polishing the mirror by hand.

He felt awkward and isolated at faculty cocktail parties where his colleagues, all of whom he regarded as intellectually superior to himself, were talking about their psychoanalyses and how they were freed from their paralyzing complexes, making them happier, more creative, more energetic and above all, more human human beings. They seemed to speak a strange language, foreign to Tom, which he later learned was Analysandese. He was stumped by its strange vocabulary, and so he felt he should not engage in conversation. He hoped that he might meet somebody who spoke Mathematics, the language of the universe, but even his mathematician colleagues preferred talking Analysandese.

He was embarrassed when the empathic Russian poet, moved by his reticence, approached him and asked him about his analysis. He lied, claiming that he was not currently in analysis because his analyst was on a two year sabbatical in Vienna. He said he was looking for another to tide him over. The Russian felt assured that this clod would be no competition to become her analyst's favorite client, and so she made the referral. (Patients want to be their analyst's best, that is, their most interesting and intelligent analysands. They try to please their analysts by making "free" associations that they know would be congruent with the interpretations of their "guide", yet leaving enough room for refinement by the analyst. For the patient to give the impression of being intellectually superior to the analyst would be a mistake, no chance at being the best.)

Tom was loaded with anxiety and ambivalence. Having overheard the conversations of his colleagues, he knew he had to lie down on Frieda's couch and start talking dreams. At two hundred dollars an hour he knew he had better talk fast. He started, "I dreamt that I was in my back yard looking through my telescope, trying to find Venus in the western sky, when out of nowhere Andromeda pops into view. I was surprised. How did she get there? She should be in the north. How could she fit in the eyepiece together with the billions of star in her galaxy? I couldn't take my eyes off of her. Suddenly, an angry stranger, wearing my father's fishing hat and carrying pruning shears appears out of nowhere and tells me that if I kept looking at Andromeda he would break my Dobsonian. He disappeared as suddenly as he appeared. I felt relieved. I woke up amused and confused. What does it mean, Doctor? What does it mean?"

"Well it's your dream, you tell me what it means," she replied nonchalantly.

Tom's arithmetical mind quickly computed that he was paying twenty dollars a word for that dumb advice. Further-more, he became more resentful when he realized that he was paying her to do battle with the censor for the release of that top secret document, the latent dream content, while she is telling him to "do it yourself". How could he? He wasn't trained. As the years passed (things move slowly in psycho-analysis) she cleverly led him through "free" association to the realization that his home-built Dobsonian symbolized an erect penis, which, like the telescope, is rigid, elongated and cylindrical and penetrates dark places, looking for an intimate relationship with a beautiful woman, Venus. He went on to associate galaxy with milk, since that is its Latin derivation, and galaxies appear milky when viewed by the naked eye or through a telescope. Further on, he associated the Andromeda constellation with a chained (married) sacrificial woman (that is the mythology) who gives milk. The angry stranger's (father's) threat to break his telescope could only mean his fear of castration for his incestuous desire for his mother. He promptly dealt with that threat by simply eliminating (killing) Dad completely from the dream. In that epiphanic session when it all came together, that sudden emotional moment of insight, he abreacted with, "OH, NO! Mamma Andromeda! Andromeda IS Mamma," and collapsed convulsively in tears as he fell off the couch.

Figure 2 This is "Mamma Andromeda". As any star gazer knows, it takes an enormous amount of imagination together with quite a few martinis to view her as she appears in this beautiful drawing.

(In the real mythological life of constellation creatures, Andromeda, who is the beautiful daughter of Cepheus and Cassiopeia, the king and queen of Ethiopia, is not yet married but is literally chained to a rock as a sacrificial gourmet meal for the sea monster, Cetus, the whale, who threatens her country. Fortunately, she is saved by Perseus, who makes her his bride, and they gallop away on Pegasus into the sunrise.)

Frieda preferred Tom's interpretation of the chained sacrificial woman, a wife/mother, which allowed her to open the door and gently guide him into the odious Oedipus complex. She granted him, shall we say, some psychoanalytic license.

Further on in his analysis, he was made aware of the "fact" that his home-built Dobsonian was not only a phallic symbol in the dream but also in real life, where he used it as a denial of his sexual inadequacy. He was extremely proud of the immense size of the instrument and boasted that it was the largest telescope in the county. In one of his sessions, Tom, at the risk of having no chance of becoming her favorite patient, was able to summon up the courage to challenge Frieda's interpretation by pointing out that he had fathered six children. She triumphantly retorted that this was further proof of the correctness of the interpretation; his telescope and fecundity indicated that he was unconsciously battling his feelings of sexual inadequacy using the ego defense mechanism of denial. (She was visibly vexed when he pointed out that Freud also had six children. As soon as he did that he knew he no longer had a chance at being her best patient.) Never having felt sexually inadequate before, Tom was feeling that way now – he felt castrated. Nevertheless, Frieda assured him that this was a sign of a successful analysis.

Analysts, all of whom are well versed in ancient Greek tragedies and constellation mythology, would nod approvingly of the interpretation that Tom had been suffering from an unresolved Oedipus complex with the attendant castration anxiety. They would agree that Frieda skillfully weakened Tom's censor by guiding his "free" associations, making his desire for the incest taboo conscious, thereby freeing up the mental energy that he was using to keep such an unacceptable wish repressed. Tom would now be a more creative, energetic, involved, interesting and most importantly, a more conversational guest at faculty cocktail parties.

Unfortunately, these good things never happened to Tom, even though his Oedipus complex, castration anxiety and sublimated, voyeuristic tendencies, a common affliction of astronomers, were analyzed and resolved. In addition, spin doctor, Frieda, interpreted his ulcer pain as the burning yearning for his mother's breast which, at one time, was his sole source of comfort and satisfaction, as it was with all of us. That interpretation, she rationalized, was proven by the temporary relief he obtained by following the (Dr.) Sippy diet, consisting of hourly gulps of milk and cream. Of course, that diet provided only temporary relief, and only successful psychoanalysis could guarantee a cure. In the twentieth year of his analysis, now in his middle sixties, Tom died of a bleeding peptic ulcer. He entered eternity bloodless and penniless but, thanks to Frieda, without a single complex. Psychoanalytic treatment can be deadly at times.

Those of the feminine gender should not feel left out or deprived of the benefits of Freudian psychology. Freud has provided them with the Electra complex and penis envy. The Electra complex is the analogue of the Oedipus complex, and sometimes it is referred to as the female Oedipus complex.

Currently, there about two dozen named complexes listed in psychiatric dictionaries. The selection is so varied that one is bound to find at least one suitable for cocktail party conversations. A clavis of these complexes includes:

Cain complex – Rivalry, competition, aggression or destructive impulses directed against a brother.

Clymestra complex – The wife who kills her husband so that she may possess one of his male relatives.

Demosthenes complex – The neurotic need to achieve mastery over inferiority feelings through words and language in the process of speaking.

Diana complex – The wish of a female to be a male.

Griselda complex – The father unconsciously, grudgingly giving up his daughter to another man.

Heracles complex – The hatred of a father for his children.

Jocasta complex – The morbid attachment of a mother for her own son.

Media complex – The hatred and or homicidal wishes of a mother toward her child.

Obscenity/purity complex – The zeal of the puritan or religious denunciation of any particular manifestation of sex is an exact measure of the intensity of its lure for such a person.

Orestes complex – A sons killing or desires to kill his own father.

Phaedra complex – A mother who is in love with her son.

If Freud were alive today and was privileged to know about neurotransmitters and the importance of their concentrations in the functions of the brain/mind, he would immediately junk his theory of latent dream content together with its censor and manifest dream content with its symbols for neurochemistry.

If one wishes to undergo psychoanalysis, the wait for the initial consultation may be fairly long since Freudian analysts are rapidly heading for extinction. Even now it is difficult to find any mention of psychoanalysis in psychiatric textbooks; it has become an historical curiosity. However, we wish for the continuing survival of those wonderful, spellbinding movies, dramas and novels where the mentally tortured, heroic analysand is rescued from a most terrible fate by the pro bono, clever analysis of an ever haunting dream by a kindly, wise, elderly analyst with a Viennese accent.

I do admire Freud's diligence in exploring dreams and appreciate his many elegant contributions to the understanding of the mind, but dream analysis is not one of them. The wart of dream analysis is still, well, a wart.

A skeptic once asked Freud about the symbolism of his panatella, to which he is said to have quipped, "A cigar is just a cigar." He had a sense of humor, and, I believe, he proposed some of his ideas with tongue as well as cigar in cheek, an unspoken word of caution to his following not to try to outfreud Freud. If, in a heavenly meeting Freud met Tom, I would hope he would bring himself to say, "It's okay, Tom, don't fret, a telescope is just a telescope."

Hall, C.S. (1953), in his search for symbols in the psychoanalytic literature, reported in *The Journal of General Psychology,* "The two most popular referents are *penis* for which there are 102 symbols, and *vagina* for which there are 95 symbols. Other referents that have a large number of symbols are *death* (62 symbols), coitus (55 symbols), *masturbation* (25 symbols), *mother* (15 symbols), *father* (14 symbols), *breasts* (13 symbols) and *castration* (12 symbols)."

If a person, with just a little bit of knowledge of Freudian symbolism makes the effort, he will be able to provide a sexual interpretation for all of his dreams. In the waking state, no matter where he looks he will notice that he is surrounded by objects that may serve as potential sexual symbols. In the glossary of this book there is an admittedly incomplete listing of some phallic symbols. If Mr. Censor allowed me to choose my own phallic symbol, I would opt for a foot long baloney, unsliced, thank you.

A Journey into Dreamland is not complementary to the old, it is a replacement for it – it is new. Freud's theory requires two *imaginings*, a latent dream and a censor. The new theory requires three *non-imaginings*: neurotransmitters, which any biologist would admit exist in reality, and, without which, any brain/mind activity is impossible, a manifest dream, which any dreamer will tell you he experiences nightly and photons, the massless quantum particles that carry the light necessary for the construction of the visual images which we experience in dreams.

Symbols are fine in religion and poetry and necessary in mathematics, but dumb in dream science. Get rid of them! Clear out your desk and pack up your symbols, latents and baloney, Mr. Censor. You're fired!

Freud smoked well over seven thousand cigars *after* he had been originally diagnosed with cancer of the mouth and jaw in 1923; at times he smoked twenty a day. He was either ignorant of or didn't care (like so many of us) about the relationship between tobacco and cancer. He died in 1939 at eighty-three. Manner of death: assisted suicide. Cause of death: morphine overdose.

Chapter 3

EINSTEIN (1879-1955)
AND THE DREAM EQUATION

"To raise new questions, new possibilities, to regard old problems from a new angle, requires creative imagination and marks real advance in science."
                                                                A. Einstein

Coincidences are amusing, and I was amused in my attempt to understand the construction of dreams. I became aware of the similarities between dream constructions and Einstein's famous $E = mc^2$. In Einstein's equation energy is constructed from mass, m, multiplied by the speed of light, c, in a vacuum, squared. (The c comes from the Latin, celeritas, meaning speed.) Dreams are constructed from memories, m, acted on by creativity, c. Increasing my amusement was the coincidence that the m in Einstein's equation was a variable that could be a ton of Uranium 235, a proton, a quark or any stuff, even the garbage that you throw out daily. The m in dreams could be the memory of a cataclysmic event in one's life or something as insignificant as a two millimeter stone.

Attempting to extract more coincidence by playing around with the c was somewhat of a failure but not a total one. In Einstein's equation c, the speed of light in a vacuum

33

is a constant, an absolute. Since his *Theory of Special Relativity* allows time to be stretched, space to be shrunk and inertial mass to be increased to infinity, and since the speed of light in a vacuum never changes under any circumstances, it may be that the speed of light may be the only genuine constant in our universe. (Recently, there has been speculation that the speed of light has been increasing with time. If that is so, it may be that there are no true constants in the universe, and what we call constants are merely useful numbers that are good enough to help us in our calculations for the time being. As theories change constants may lose their usefulness.) Certainly the c of creativity is not a constant, and I suspect that there are no mental phenomena that could possibly be regarded as constants since we have no rulers, clocks or scales that can measure them as absolutes. But there is one thing we can safely say about the c of creativity; like the speed of light, if it could be measured, it would be a very large number. In no way could I coincide the ^{2} in Einstein's equation with the dream equation, so I settled for the indefinite ^{n}, which is whatever number yet to be discovered. Believe me, it will never be discovered. Keep in mind that creativity is not just an addition to memory to make a dream (not $D = m + c^n$), but it must act on memory to give the product, D, and therefore, the dream equation must be $D = m \times c^n$.

The similarity between Einstein's $E = mc^2$ and $D = mc^n$ is obvious, and I admit to some petty plagiarizing here. However, if Einstein were still alive I would hope that he would concede that I have as much right to use the alphabet as he has, without attribution to that self-educated genius of geniuses who invented it. Unarguably, the alphabet is the greatest invention of all time; imagine a world without it or even only without its vowels.

Einstein's equation explains how, at the beginning of creation, energy was transformed into mass. We see the result, our universe. His equation also shows that mass can be changed into energy, very useful for our survival. Without a doubt, such construction and dissection of his equation is of immense usefulness. As we focus on each member of Einstein's equation, we can see that a small amount of mass can produce a huge amount of energy by virtue of the large number that c represents (300,000 kilometers/sec. or 186,200 miles/ sec.). Analogously, in the dream equation, we see the product of memory and creativity. Memory is the small component and consists of one or many important or unimportant past experiences, while creativity is the large and powerful number that creates the wonderfully mysterious phenomenon of dreaming. $D = mc^n$ can be dissected in a manner similar to the dissection of $E = mc^2$. It takes just a tiny bit of memory to produce a dream because human creativity is so great.

At first, one may think, "So what if $D = mc^n$, who cares?" Consider these possibilities: just as Einstein's equation led to the invention of the atomic bomb and other more beneficial inventions for mankind, $D = mc^n$ may lead to some significant treatments for serious mental disorders such as psychoses and dementia. Dreams are similar to the diagnostic symptoms of psychosis which include delusions, hallucinations and bizarre behavior. Now, being that dreams are so similar to psychosis, if we rewrite the equation as P (psychosis) $= mc^n$, we may be able to apply it to some psychiatric patients. For example, patients who suffer from bipolar disorder (manic depressive illness), and are in a manic state, are treated with lithium carbonate. These patients are frequently at the high end of creativity. They complain that lithium, although it may rid them of their grandiose delusions and hallucinations and allows them to function, it also diminishes their creativity. If that is so, it may be that lithium exerts its therapeutic effect by decreasing creativity during dreaming and the waking state, resulting in a decrease in psychotic symptoms. This suggests that in the treatment of bipolar disorder we should focus our search for drugs that purposefully decrease creativity. Unfortunately that would be a trade-off that would be difficult to accept.

Another possibility to be considered is in the treatment of dementia, the primary symptom of which is memory impairment. If, in our dream equation, we increase dreaming and creativity remains the same then the equation tells us that memory will increase. Others and I have tried it and found it to be true that the drug, Aricept and other acetyl-cholinesterase inhibitors which are used in the treatment of dementia, increase dreaming or, at least, increase the ability to remember dreams. (A number of years ago, because of my interest in dreams and remembering them, I began taking Aricept 5 mg. at bedtime. Not experiencing the desired effect, I stopped using it. About one year ago I tried again at the higher dose of 10 mg. with remarkable success. My dreams became more complicated, and my memory of dreams increased from about one every other night to up to three remembered dreams a night.) One of the adverse reactions listed in the *Physician's Desk Reference* for Aricept is nightmares. Although I have never experienced night-mares while taking Aricept, my dreams, for the most part, were distinctly unpleasant, and, awakening with memories of complicated dreams, left me exhausted instead of refreshed. In addition, Aricept has the tendency to cause urinary incontinence in elderly gentlemen. Because we are now aware of the relationship $D = mc^n$, we can see that we can manipulate the variables in the equation with medication.

Dreaming is impossible without memory and creativity; creativity times zero memory makes no dream; memory times zero creativity makes no dream. Memory alone is a photograph; memory acted on by creativity is a video, is a dream.

An even more remarkable coincidence is the similarity of dream contents to Einstein's *Theory of Special Relativity*, which I had previously stated includes the stretching (slowing) of time, the shrinking of space and the increase in inertial mass. The absolutes of time, space and inertial mass turn into relatives proportional to the speed of travel compared to the speed of light.

Imagine that the two dots enclosed in the brackets represent two tics of a clock one second apart under normal conditions: [. .]. Now imagine that these two dots again enclosed in brackets represent two tics of the same clock one second apart while traveling at 90% of the speed of light: [.   .] This is an illustration of the stretching of time which is one of the components of *Einstein's Special Theory of Relativity.*

In the year 3000, NASA, having perfected the technology that allows space travel at the speed of light, sends a thirty year old astronaut on a fly-by mission to Alpha Centauri Proxima, which is about four light years away. During the journey, as expected, the time on the mission clocks is stretched one hundred fold, so that one second in mission time is one hundred seconds in down on earth time, and one year in mission time is one hundred years in earth time, making travel to distant galaxies at least theoretically possible. When we talk about mission clocks traveling at the speed of light we are referring to all clocks whether they are water clocks, mechanical clocks, digital clocks, atomic clocks and, most importantly, biological clocks. Under the conditions stated above, (186,200 mi./sec.), they will all tic slower. As the result of the slowing of time, the biological clocks responsible for the heart beat, respiration, metabolic functions and aging would all be decelerated. Most peculiar is that on such a mission our astronaut is unaware of time being stretched, even though his ability to do much more work is increased – he can now count to a hundred in one second. To better enhance your grasp of time stretching, dwell briefly on how it would be if there was time shrinking.

The astronaut, returning to earth eight time-stretched years later (four years going and four returning), finds that the calendar now reads 3800 A.D. The landscape is changed, relatives, friends and colleagues are all dead, and he is now eight hundred and thirty years old. How can that be, and what does it have to do with dreams? I don't know how that can be, but we frequently experience time stretching in dreams.

In dreams, more frequently than not, we move at the speed of light so that in .0367 seconds we may find our-selves 6,837 miles moved from our bed, standing in the nude in front of a cheering crowd of one hundred thousand in Yankee Stadium in Beijing, China, accepting the Nobel Prize in Literature for our recipe for hot dogs and beans. Obviously, we were able to make such a long trip for this momentous occasion in such a short period of time only if time was stretched. In dreams we do it with the greatest of ease, and with the same lack of awareness as the astronaut.

A curious phenomenon is the feeling of time *shrinking* as a function of the aging process, the opposite of Einstein's time being stretched when traveling toward the speed of light. It is recognizable at almost any age but mostly exper-ienced by the elderly; "I was just five, now, suddenly, I'm eighty five." Any geezer will tell you that it only seems like yesterday that he starred in baseball, dated pretty girls or was on Omaha beach on D-day. It is an illusion, of course. The velocity of time does not change with age – a second is a second, a month is a month, and a year remains a year. Theories include:

• There is an area of the brain whose job it is to recognize the passage of time which gradually fails with aging.

• It may have to do with proportionality, that is, at five years of age, one year is one fifth of one's lifetime, while at eighty years, one year is one eightieth of one's lifetime, creating the illusion of the acceleration of time.

• With aging movement is slowed; it takes a longer time to do things, producing the same illusion of time shrinking.

According to Einstein's *Theory of Special Relativity* the passage of time does not vary with aging or anything else except when we approach the speed of light. The illusion of time stretching is a nightly occurrence for the insomniac. How can 8 A.M. be so far removed from 2 A.M. An eighty-five year old insomniac, and I am speaking from my own experience, is doubly afflicted by the illusions of day time shrinking and night time stretching of time. Whatever the cause of the illusion, I don't like it.

Another component of Einstein's *Special Theory of Relativity* is the shrinking of space. While they are traveling in a rocket ship, say, at 90% of the speed of light, imagine that your mother is sitting in the front seat and your wife is seated ten feet behind. Special relativity tells us that at that speed the space separating your mother from your wife will shrink in the direction of travel so that Mommy might end up sitting on wife's lap or even occupying the same skin. We all have had the experience of identifying an individual in a dream as being two different persons at the same time. Was it Mom or was it my wife? Space has shrunk. A photographer with a high tech camera took the picture enclosed in the brackets of Mom and wife speeding by, at first at $1/1000^{th}$ of the speed of light $[>^wO==O^m>]$. Then he took another picture when they were moving at 90% of the speed of light $[>^wO^m>]$.

The shrinking of space produces not only the multiple personality type of individual described above but also a merging of places; was that dream about my high school graduation or my wedding?

With any movement, no matter how slight, in any direction (velocity) we are approaching the speed of light and time is being stretched. (I am not saying that such movement is close to the speed of light – far from it.)

Simultaneously, there must be a corresponding, proportional shrinking of space, or else there will be a warp in the fabric of spacetime. Dreams lack that necessary simultaneity, and consequently, *dreams are the mental equivalents of warps in the fabric of spacetime.* That's what makes dreams crazy and recognizable as dreams. See Figure 3. The warping is complicated, it doesn't look like a simple, single warp that we ordinarily see in fabrics. That is because it is a combination of multiple successive warps, warps upon warps that occur as the result of rapid changing of the concentrations of neurotransmitters that result in rapid changing of the memories as they are released to us in dreams.

It is difficult to find coherence in dreams, but there is some which we fail to notice because it is masked by so much incoherence. Say, we have a dream of the grammar school we attended seventy five years ago. We experience memories of the classroom, the building itself, the candy store down the street and the vicious pit bully, Nero, who would guarantee that any child, daring to walk to school by his property, would not be left with dry pants. The coherence we see here is coherence of place. The contents of this dream are limited to a certain locality that is memorable, that being the area that is in proximity to the school. Surprisingly, dreams seem to hold this coherence. We seldom, if ever would start the dream at the school and pop up in Beijing, but it would not be unusual to be in the fourth grade classroom and suddenly pop up in the nearby candy store without any intervening space or time. There appear to be memory compartments in our temporal lobes that maintain some orderliness and connectedness for spatial memories. Places in our dreams may be familiar, semi-familiar or unfamiliar. Our exposure to the many venues on TV may be responsible for those that seem unfamiliar. This unfamiliarity is a testament to the unimportance of dream content.

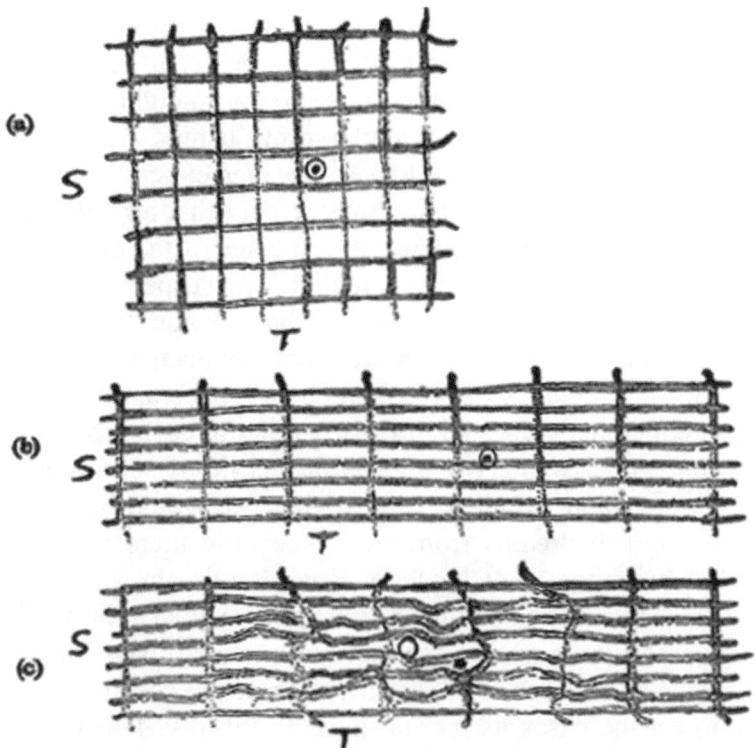

Figure 3 The fabric of spacetime. (a) This is the way you experience it while reading this book. (b) An astronaut travels near the speed of light where time is stretched and space is shrunk, but he experiences it as (a); he doesn't notice anything unusual. (c) For you as a dreamer, time is stretched and space is shrunk, as it is for the astronaut, but there is a huge warp in the fabric, and, like the astronaut, you don't notice anything unusual; you experience it as (a) until you wake up and recognize the craziness. The circles and dots represent the relationship between space and time as they are perceived in the three different modes of awareness.

In a similar manner, if in the beginning of a dream, we are a certain age, we remain at that age throughout the dream. In dreams, we don't skip from eighty to ten or vice versa, even though it's not appropriate for an eighty year old to be sitting in a fourth grade classroom behind a desk built for a ten year old. The old man dreamer experiences it as real and recognizes nothing strange about that arrangement. So, in dreams, we see coherence in the age of the dreamer at whatever age. Also in this situation we suspect compartments in our temporal lobes that have some function at keeping our age memories in order and connected.

So, in dreams, we see coherence of space and time, but those coherences run like threads parallel to each other; they are not properly interwoven like the fabric of spacetime. If they were, there would be times when we would be unable to distinguish dreams from reality because there would be no law breaking. See Chapter 8, Erwin's ? dream.

The third component of Einstein's special relativity is the increase in inertial mass (not gravitational mass) that we experience in dreams. When traveling at the speed of light, an object increases its inertial mass to infinity. This doesn't mean that there is an increase in stuff or weight of the object. It means that nothing can move it from its trajectory because there is nothing faster than the speed of light, and to do that would require something traveling faster than light speed. It would be similar for a person whose top speed is ¼ mile a minute (a four minute miler) to attempt to push a car traveling faster than fifteen miles an hour (i.e., ¼ of a mile a minute). The faster something is moving the more difficult it becomes to accelerate it, and once it reaches the speed of light further acceleration becomes impossible. The inertial mass has increased to infinity. If, in a dream, we are being pursued by some evil predator, the faster we try to run (accelerate) the heavier our legs become. We become lead legged, not because the stuff in our legs has increased in amount or weight, but because the faster we speed acceleration becomes more difficult and eventually impossible. Hopefully, at this point we will wake up, but screaming.

The three elements of Einstein's *Theory of Special Relativity* reveal themselves in dreams. In addition, Einstein's ideas, like dreams, are pretty crazy, and like Freud, he made them even crazier. (The difference between the two was that Einstein proved his crazy ideas mathematically.) He claimed that those people who would be involved in all that speeding around close to the speed of light would have no idea that anything unusual was happening, that time was being stretched, space was being shrunk and that inertial mass was being increased to infinity; only an outside observer would be witness to these strange happenings. How similar this is to our dreams. We are unimpressed when we are involved in crazy dream action; it is only when we awaken and become outside observers of our dream memory that we recognize its craziness.

Freud and Einstein were contemporaries. They met briefly in Berlin in 1927. The meeting was probably not collegial. Why they met, and what transpired during the meeting is unclear. It may have had something to do with Einstein's eldest son, Eduard, who suffered from schizophrenia and was hospitalized at the Burgholzli, a famous psychiatric hospital in Zurich, or it may have been Einstein's curiosity about his famous "bovine" dream that opened the door to relativity. Each of these geniuses had little respect for the other's contributions to science. This was especially true of Einstein, who berated Freud's psychoanalysis. Apparently, Freud was a little less demeaning stating, "Einstein understands about as much about psychology, as I do of physics." Both were loaded with intellectual pride. Both caused revolutions. Freud became king of the mind. Einstein became king of matter. Their meeting occurred when psychoanalysis and relativity were at their zeniths. The eyes of the world were on both. They seemed to battle over intellectual superiority like two fifth graders competing for recognition as being the smartest kid in the class. With time, Einstein won out. He proved it with mathematics.

In 1933, setting aside their antagonism, they began an extensive communication by mail, and they eventually collaborated on the pamphlet, *Why War?*, expressing their ideas about war and peace. Einstein, the pacifist, was confident that a body such as *The League of Nations* could solve the war problem, but he felt that it lacked the clout to enforce its decisions on the disputes between nations. Paradoxically, he felt that such an international organization required an army to keep the peace by waging war. (The current *U.N.* has a peace keeping military force.) Freud, on the other hand, was pessimistic that there was any solution to the war problem in view of the fact that man and other animals are endowed with both sexual and aggressive drives, the first directed toward the survival of the species, while the latter is directed toward the survival of the individual or the aggregate of individuals, as in nations.

Einstein died at seventy six in 1955 of a ruptured aorta. He was cremated, and the whereabouts of his ashes has been a well-kept secret. They may have been scattered or may all remain in one place. The remainder of his brain (that is that part that has not been distributed to pathologists for study) is at Princeton Hospital.

Unfortunately, his relatives who were not wealthy were also not entrepreneurial. They could have gotten big bucks for a lock of his electrified hair, (he had hair to spare.) or small pinches of his ashes together with certificates of authenticity. There seems to be a hot market for stuff like that, considering that Bernie Madoff's undies were auctioned off to some fool for thousands of dollars.

Chapter 4

MEMORIES

"We are our memories."
Anon

Memories, not fingerprints or DNA, are what distinguish us from every other individual on the planet. They are uniquely our memories. Our memories are us. We are a bundle of remembered faces, places and experienced life events that make us different from all other individuals that exist, ever existed or ever will exist. (Let's not get into that parallel universe stuff that claims we may also exist as our other selves in another universe. Let's stick to the gorgeous universe we know.) Many of us wonder if we will maintain our memories and, therefore, our identities in heaven or will we just melt into God.

In dreams we are not only aware of our existence, but know who we are. We supply our exclusive lifetime memories that make up the stories in our dreams. Our dream selves which is the way we were, (because dreams are memories they are always past tense) and our waking selves which is the way we are unified in dreams; there is no multiple personality there. You are the very same person now as the child you see in your dreams although fifty years may have intervened. Later on this will be claimed as an important secondary utility of dreams.

In addition to fixing (forming) our personality, memory is our obedient servant except in dreams. In the waking state, we command it to retrieve from its vast files of events of the past, and it does it. It usually serves us well enough but not necessarily perfectly. It helps us to get through life. If we lose it, survival becomes impossible unless some caring person or institution comes along to the rescue. Memory does not serve us well in dreams, it is an uncontrollable rogue. We have no control over the memories or their sequencing that we experience in dreams, which is, for the most part, illogical. But it does serve us well enough for the task of dreaming, which is to make us aware of our existence even when we sleep. In dreams, memory doesn't have to be accurate although it may be, it doesn't have to be detailed, although it may be, it doesn't have to be colored, although it may be, and it doesn't have to be emotional although it may be. The thing it has to be is powerful enough to awaken us from the dead (non-dream) sleep, making us aware that we exist and who we are.

Memories are indispensable in the construction of dreams. Remember in the dream equation if there is no "m" there is no "D". Thought dreams may be an exception.

The cognitive functions of the brain are thinking, perceiving and remembering, all of which are identifiable in both the waking and dream states. Unlike perceiving, which is a purely passive function in the awake and dream states, remembering is an active function in the awake state and purely passive when we are dreaming. (In dreams we don't choose our memories. They are forced upon us.) Thinking is an active function when we are dreaming and when we are awake. The thinking we do when we are dreaming is as good, logical and reliable as it is when we are awake. This is surprising considering the craziness we are immersed in during dreaming. Not everything about dreams is crazy. The three cognitive functions remain operative in dreams. No wonder we have that feeling of "being there".

The following is a humorous autobiographical narrative that demonstrates how dream stories are constructed. It is the story of "stories" which, I believe, is a simple but excellent analogy that illustrates the relationship between memories and creativity: When I was a boy, about the time when families were able to afford their first radios, we played a game, or more precisely, it was a pastime called "stories". We learned it from our older cousin, thirteen at the time, who gave it up because, at that level of maturity, he considered everything dumb. My friends, who were mainly maternal cousins, were all pre-teen and younger. Each of us made a list of about ten items, which came to a total of about forty or fifty; they were things that frequently came up in the conversations of kids at that age at that time. They might include: The Yankees, Jack Armstrong, Red Ryder BB guns, brazeers [*Sic*], sling shots, God, Victor the cop, President Roosevelt, Sister Mary Pancratius, Limburg [*Sic*], pee pee (the all-time number one favorite), Joe Louis, Babe Ruth, Kotex, Dick Tracy, Nero, pee pee, root beer and grape chewing gum, dragons, Shirley Temple, Uncle Waller, pee pee, Hitler, Amelia Airhart [*Sic*], Grampa's cherry tree, two wheelers, the end of the world, Dracula, sins, the devil and many others, all nouns. We then wrote them down on individually torn scraps of paper, rolled them into marble-sized balls and placed them in a baseball cap. Each one of us would take turns at picking ten of them, and then we would attempt to compose a story, most of the time humorous, sometimes scary, using the picked words. Usually Stashek, who was the youngest, was the first to start. (We delighted in teaching him "bad" words and, of course, when confronted by his Mommy, we all lied.)

"Victor, the cop, knocked on my door. I opened the door. He was wearing a brassiere. (Rolling on the floor laughter.) He said he came to arrest me for shooting a hole in Mr. Voytek's window with my Red Ryder. He said he would take my gun away from me. I was scared, and did pee pee in my pants. He said I was a bad boy, and he was going to tell Sister Mary Pancratius on me, and she would hit me with her ruler, and then, then, then she came to my house in an Electra with Amelia Earhart. She was wearing a Kotex. (Stashek, being the youngest, about eight, was not our equal in sophistication or in knowledge of reproductive physiology. He thought that Kotex was some kind of coat. Consequently, he was bewildered and pleasantly surprised by more rolling on the floor laughter. He enjoyed his comedic stardom.) I was crying, but then Shirley Temple showed up on her purple two-wheeler, and, and, and she said she liked me." Clap, clap, clap and more claps. Needless to say, Stashek always hoped to pick Kotex again to enjoy, once more, the rousing appreciation of his audience. Then Edziu, then Bobby, then Jashek had their turns, all creatively adding verbs to make a story. Who cared if it was goofy, it was fun. We don't engage in that pastime anymore except in dreams.

Stashek had more control over the contents of his story than we have over our dreams. He could, using his free will, supply specific verbs to the nouns forced upon him by the rules of the "stories" pastime. In dreams, we not only have to accept the memories given to us by neurotransmitters, but we also have to accept the actions forced on the memories by the concentrations of their molecules.

"Lucid dreams" resemble day dreams because the will is operative in the selection of memories and creativities. Because of the strong feeling of "being there", they also resemble ordinary dreams. They are best described as *super day dreams*. They are not ordinary dreams, although ordinary dreams are used to get to that state of lucidity. In lucid dreaming there is extraordinary involvement in *chosen* dream content which we often experience in deep daydreams. Most of us have had the experience of waking up from a pleasant dream, and we wanted it to continue, and we were able to do

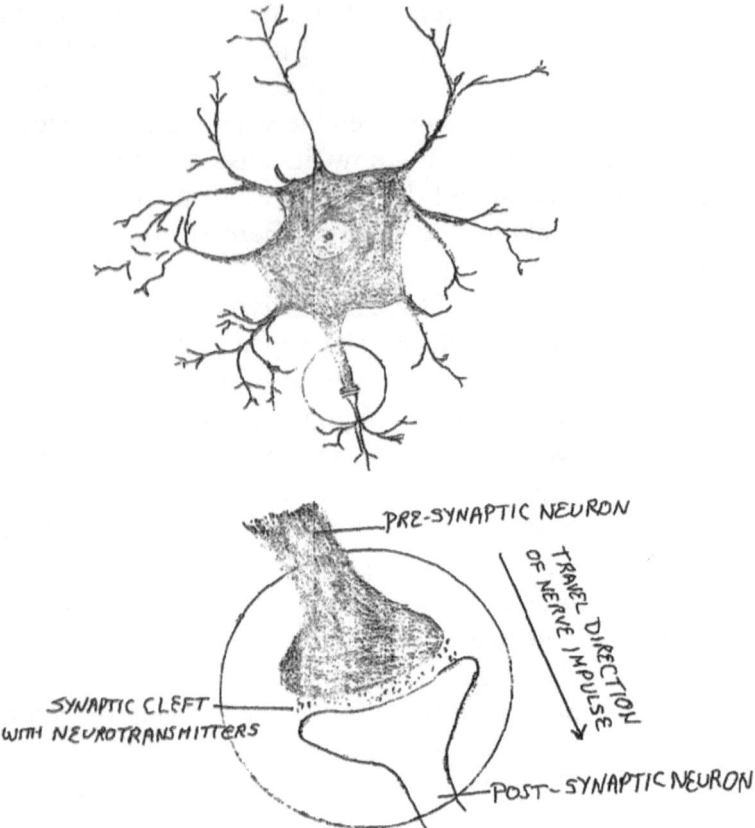

Figure 4 Top – A neuron with one of its many synapses in chemical contact with another neuron.
Bottom – A magnified illustration of the above encircled synapse with its neurotransmitters.

Dualism states that mind and brain are two distinct entities that interact somehow. Rene Descartes (1596-1650) proposed that mind lived in the brain and, most specifically, lived in that part of the brain which we call the "Cartesian Theater", which he claimed was located in the pineal gland. Apparently, he decided to build his theater in the pineal gland because it is an unpaired structure located between the two cerebral hemispheres, an ideal location for his theater crowd. His idea was that the mind sat in the one seat theater, where it was presented with perceptions that allowed it to make judgments and give commands by way of the will. Certainly, this was a far from satisfactory explanation for the relationship between mind and body but much more acceptable than materialism.

One Mind is bizarre. It states that matter does not exist, only mind, *one* mind, *your* mind, and that mind creates the illusion of matter. It denies the material existence of the book you are now reading, and it claims, that this book is the product of your mind not mine, since I and all the other authors you have ever read are brainless and, of course, mindless. It claims that there is only your mind in all of non-existing creation; whatever you perceive exists only in your mind, whoever you are. The universe you see was created by you. It mildly resembles lucid dreaming. If one becomes a serious believer in this philosophy, he cannot resist the grand feeling of omnipotence reserved for God alone. Consequently, such a belief could bring one to the brink of insanity and perhaps, even cause one to end up in a mental institution.

There appear to be some clues as to where mind meets body at the microscopic level. Each cell in our bodies contains organelles known as mitochondria. Mitochondria are bacteria or organelles that so closely resemble bacteria that it doesn't matter what you believe they are. They live symbiotically within us. We provide them with shelter and oxygen, and they provide us with energy. Mommies pass them from generation to generation. Although Dad's sperm cells also contain mitochondria, they are left outside when his sperm penetrates the egg. It is the mitochondria that have the ability to make new synapses between neurons and act together with neurotransmitters as gatekeepers that open memory gates when we tell them to. However, in dreams they ignore our requests and open the gates that they want to open.

Mitochondria are terrific; we can't live without them. Unfortunately, the byproducts of their activity are oxidants, poisons that eventually kill their host cells and themselves, a case of murder/suicide.

(Elderly people who engage in intellectual and memory challenging activities, either on the job or through pastimes such as reading, crosswords, cards, etc., are more likely to delay or prevent dementia because the mitochondria are stimulated to make new synapses that facilitate memory and learning.)

Since dreams are deprived of will and we are totally powerless over what we dream, the haphazard, incoherent presentation of memories by the mitochondria and neurotransmitters are uncorrectable. But that's O.K. because that kind of craziness is necessary. If the craziness wasn't there, how would we know we were dreaming? The lack of will in dreams also absolves us from the guilt we would normally experience when we break moral or civil laws in the waking state.

The uncertainty associated with memories in dreams (as in Heisenberg's *Uncertainty Principle*) popping into and out of existence suggests that they should be called quantum memories. They mimic the mysterious behavior of quantum particles. Dreams are frequently forgotten immediately on waking. Those that are remembered generally have a short memory life span, and all that remains is the memory of having dreamed but no memory of content. This occurs physiologically because of the uncontrolled, rapidly changing concentrations of neurotransmitters, which open and close the gates of the memory neurons and practically, because *memories of dream content are unimportant.*

If a dreamer is awakened while screaming during a nightmare, the memory of that dream content is extremely brief even though he may make an extraordinary effort to recall it. If he is not awakened while screaming during the nightmare and the dream is allowed to continue, there is usually no memory of dream content and even no memory that the dream occurred. The dreamer only knows it when his bed mate tells him about it in the morning. And even that information neither brings to memory the dream content nor having had the dream.

One of the symptoms (criteria) of post-traumatic stress disorder (PTSD), aside from the deliberate attempts to forget the traumatic event, is the involuntary inability to recall important aspects of the trauma. The horror part frequently has not been deposited in the memory bank. When nightmares are allowed to continue without being awakened, the amnesia is similar to the amnesia that is experienced in PTSD. Why should that occur? Perhaps Mother Nature, in her beneficence, is sparing us from being revisited by the terror of what we experienced in the dream.

Although memories of past events, faces and places, remote and recent, are important in constructing dreams, remembering content, which may be interesting and entertaining, is a waste of good mental energy. Any kind of memory can do what is necessary to make a dream, just as any kind of mass will do to make energy, and any kind of exercise will do to improve our cardiovascular health, assuming one is not interested in the aesthetics of pecs, abs and glutes. *It is the act of dreaming that is important, not the dream content.*

Most frequently, in dreams, recent and remote memories are presented and experienced pretty much simultaneously which supports the craziness of dreams by breaking the laws governing the sequencing of time. How can what happened years ago be happening at the same time as what happened yesterday? Is this a time warp in the fabric of spacetime?

In dreams we experience familiar memories. We recognize them without difficulty, but we also experience memories that are unfamiliar. The memories that we experience while awake or dreaming are bare-bones memories and are, for the most part, accurate, but when we apply creativity to them, they may become unrecognizable. For example, one may remember making a guided tour of Italy in 2000, but comparing memorable experiences with your traveling companion a few years later, there is little correlation in the details. It is as if you were in two different tourist groups. So it is in dreams. The dreamer's unique creativity, which, as we said before, is applied automatically without the consent of the dreamer, hangs meaty memories, inaccurate in detail on the accurate bare-bones memories, causing feelings of unfamiliarity.

In addition, memories are inherently unstable; they fade with time unless they are periodically refreshed. Just as it does with matter, the law of entropy (the second law of thermodynamics) governs memories. They change with time in the direction of disorder and eventually, after creativity does its job on them, they may defy recognition. If you visit the grammar school that you attended fifty years ago, which was such an important part of your life for nine years, you will be surprised how different your memory of it is from the way it exists fifty years later in reality. Your memory of it has entropied, and when you wake up from a dream constructed with such an entropied memory it will take great effort to recognize that dream image as your old grammar school. Similarly, the usual memory that we might have of a nicely layered and easily identifiable ingredients of the cheeseburger with bacon, lettuce, tomato, onion and mayo, that we had enjoyed for lunch, may turn into an unrecognizable, disordered blob of something questionably edible on a hard roll in our dream. More remarkable and enigmatic, when we awaken and remember the dream, we reverse entropy by reorganizing and reinterpreting the blob as the original visual memory of the cheeseburger with the works, layered and easily identifiable. But it makes no difference that it has been disordered with entropy since *it is the dreaming that is important not the dream content.* The entropy of the memories that we experience in dreams is significantly more rapid than that which we experience in the waking state. As we grow older such entropic dream experiences become increasingly more common.

Jamais vu is an interesting phenomenon that most of us have experienced. We have lived in the same house for many years, we are away for one week, and when we return, we have a strange feeling of unfamiliarity in this very familiar setting that is surprising and, fortunately, passes within minutes. This experience in the waking state attests to the instability of memories, which, with little effort, can be corrected but are uncorrectable when we are dreaming. The stranger in the dream is your uncle Stanley, the memory of whose face has been changed by seventy intervening years. He has been jamais vued.

More amazing is déjà vu, a feeling of familiarity that occurs in a non-familiar setting. It is as if one is experiencing exactly what one has experienced before, almost to the point of being able to predict what is about to happen. It is like what has passed has become present. The arrow of time has been reversed; we experience time backwards. The feeling does not seem to be triggered by current perceptions, although one Freudian analyst, Ferenczi, was able to trace that feeling of familiarity, experienced by one of his patients to the patient's dream.

On the one hand, déjà vu is less than a memory. It is the *feeling* of a memory without content. On the other hand, it is more than a memory in that in memories the content is there, but we do not experience the *feeling* of happening again (being there). Similarly, if we compare, say, the memories of our high school graduation when we are awake with the memories of the same event in a dream, we find that in the awake state, where our memories are more accurate and consequently, provide us with a more realistic recollection, we do not get that feeling of "being there" again that we get in dreams where we are using grossly inaccurate, deteriorated so by lying still and concentrating on the dream content. It is obvious that in such a situation we use our will, and if we are successful in doing that, it is because we are in a state of consciousness that does not resemble what we experience in ordinary dreams, and we know it. Just as there are no choices in gravity and all the other laws of nature, we have no choices in picking our dreams. *There is no free will in dreams.*

In all dreams and in all mental activity neurotransmitters are in charge. See Figure 4. The concentrations of neuro-transmitters are not fixed; influenced by many factors, they vary. When we are awake, through the power of our will, we can, for the most part, retrieve whatever memory we want. This is accomplished through the never to be understood interaction between psyche and soma. How can there be an interaction between that which is immaterial and that which is matter? Philosophers have grappled with this problem for millennia. Currently, they offer three theories: Materialism, Dualism and One Mind. Materialism solves the problem by getting rid of mind; One Mind solves the problem by getting rid of matter; Dualism accepts the existence of mind and matter, but that brings us to no greater under-standing of that unique interaction. It just tells us that they interact.

Materialism tells us that everything is matter, that there is no mind, only brain. Consequently, matter can only inter-act with matter, which means that everything is predeter-mined and cannot be changed by the act of a non-existent will. What we experience as volition is just atoms and mole-cules behaving in their predetermined way, i.e., following the physical laws of nature. That is a theory hard to swallow since we know through experience that we can freely choose through an act of the will, to move or not to move, to remember or not to remember, to remember this or to remem-ber that.

memories of that event. We conclude that the feelings of reality that we experience in our dreams are not related to the accuracy of our memories. "Being there" in a dream is, to use the most famous of Yogiisms, "déjà vu all over again".

Many of us have experienced what we believe to be repeated dreams. Considering the unpredictability of the concentrations of neurotransmitters from minute to minute, it is difficult to imagine that neurotransmitters in their proper concentration are able to organize themselves in such a way as to produce accurate repetitions of previous dreams. It is more likely that the so called repeated dream is a manifestation of a déjà vu experience. We have the feeling of having been in that dream before.

The temporal lobes of the brain are recognized as the main repositories for memories. People who suffer from temporal lobe epilepsy, i.e., when abnormal electrical discharges originate in the temporal lobes, have a variety of memory problems including frequent episodes of jamais vu and déjà vu. Whereas the average individual has no problem in determining if an event happened or they dreamed it, the temporal lobe epileptic might encounter considerable difficulty.

I was surprised to discover, what should have long been obvious, that almost all memories used in the construction of dreams are visual, and rightly so, since our main contact with the outside world is visual. Rarely, there may be a brief inclusion of one of the other senses. I urge the readers to examine their dreams carefully to see if this is a valid observation. In remembered dreams I have never experienced sound, smell or taste. On two occasions I dreamed touch. The absence of sound, at first glance, is hard to believe since we all have experienced verbal communication in dreams. While awake the most common source of communication is through sound waves produced by spoken words. In dreams we exchange ideas not through the medium of sound waves but by telepathic communication (mental telepathy), not difficult to believe since we are communicating with ourselves; one part of the brain is communicating with another part of the same brain. Occasionally, an extraneous sound, such as a ringing alarm clock, is incorporated into a dream, but that is not a memory of a sound, it is, in fact, a bona fide sound. There is also the absence of smell memories in a dream, but yet, if there is a fire we might incorporate the odor of real smoke into the dream. The same applies to taste and touch.

Admittedly, this is a peculiar arrangement, but where could sound waves, taste and smell molecules come from to produce these perceptions in dreams? They can't come from anywhere, that's why we don't experience them in dreams. The next obvious question is, "Well, where does the light come from that forms the images in our dreams, being that we are sleeping with our eyes closed in a totally dark room, while dreaming of lying on a Caribbean beach on a Sun soaked day?"

Photons come directly from the Sun or artificial sources (e.g., light bulbs) and bounce off external objects at specific frequencies and into our retinas, eventually ending up producing electrical impulses that travel from our eyes to the back of the brain where they are interpreted as outside objects with specific forms and colors. Certainly, the photons that produce the light images in dreams are not coming from outside of us. They have been bound and stored in chemical molecules within us and are released when they are needed as in the construction of visual dream images. It is likely that in dreams the chemicals that produce photons that make up the visual memories become depleted after about five to twenty minutes, at which point the lights go out, and the dream is ended.

Individuals who have acquired blindness are deprived of visual images in the waking state but they experience the visual images and memories while dreaming as does the sighted person and as they did prior to the onset of their blindness. The photons come out of storage. What makes them come out of storage? The answer awaits in the final chapter.

If Freud knew about neurotransmitters what we know of them today, how they worked in producing the memories that dreams are made of, he would have dumped his dream theory without hesitation. (He was selling his complexes and interpretations just as neurotransmitters were being discovered.) It is the concentration of neurotransmitters at the synapses of neurons that are not only responsible for dream content but also for dream amnesia. Most likely, content is determined by increasing concentrations, amnesia determined by decreasing concentration. In dreams, when the concentrations of the neurotransmitters reach an optimal level, they open the gates to the involuntary recall of memories. Most often, that task being completed, the neurotransmitter concentrations are significantly decreased, and the gates to those dream memories are totally or partially closed causing complete or incomplete amnesia for the dream content. More often than not, it happens that no matter how determined the effort, the recall fails.

Chapter 5

CREATIVITY

"And created man to His own image."
Genesis 1:27

Creation is making something out of nothing. Creativity is making something out of something. Creation is God's job. He supplies the raw material, the known elements of the periodic table and those yet to be discovered. Better yet, He supplied Lemaitre's primeval atom, and left creativity to man.

The deists among us hear God say, "I am now retired. I have given you everything you need for survival. I am leaving Mother Nature in charge. Now don't bother me!" The theists hear God say, "I am now retiring, but I am always available for consultation, if you run into a problem get in touch." The atheist is deaf. (In case you are wondering about me, I am mostly a deist from Monday through Saturday and a theist on Sunday, but trying to be a theist seven days a week.)

Creation benefits *all* mankind; the benefits of creativity are severely limited to a specific group or area. Since there is a certain similarity between creation and creativity, some people believe that when *The Bible* states that man is made in the image of God it is referring to that similarity, our little taste of godliness. However, no matter what degree of creativity we succeed in achieving, it can never be comparable to the miracle of creation.

To make his life more pleasant and ensure his survival, God has given man the gift of creativity which separates him from all other living creatures. Cave man creatively fashions a club out of a tree branch to protect himself and his family from vicious predators, thereby surviving himself and contributing to the gene pool that will guarantee the survival of his species. The creativity of the biological scientist allows us to survive the ever stalking, predatory bacteria and viruses that are eager to send us prematurely to our graves. When Homo sapiens first populated the earth, creativity was directed at survival. With time and increasing security, creativity has more and more focused on comfort and pleasure. However, there are still a lot of good, creative brains out there that are focused on survival, preparing for the inevitable collision of a huge asteroid with planet Earth.

When we are awake, a good deal of our time is occupied in creativity, ways to make our lives easier and more pleasant. However, as you know, creativity is not limited to waking life; it is pervasive in our dreams. Remember, without creativity there is no dream. Without Stashek's creativity there would just be a bunch of nouns scribbled on scraps of paper, not the fun story he attempts to create.

There is a relationship between intelligence and creativity where, for the most part, creativity is directly proportional to intelligence. This appears to be true, but I am sure there are numerous instances of very intelligent individuals who are short on creativity and creative people who are not very intelligent. An additional quantifying factor for creativity is life experience. Creativity is a child born of the union of intelligence and life experience. Creativity and intelligence increase proportionally to the number of neurons we are gifted with and the number of synapses we construct during the course of our lives. An infant's dream, we would expect to be simple. At first it might be about the breast that satisfies its hunger and later on of the smiling face of its mother. When a three year old is asked what she dreamed, the reply might be, "a wittle wed wabbit". Further questioning might reveal that the wittle wed wabbit was wunning. With time and the inevitable increase in life experiences, family, friends, classmates, teachers, neighbors, things and places will form the visual memories in her dreams to which will be imparted more and more complicated actions or plots depending on her creativity.

If dream content is unimportant, as I have previously stated, why is all that creativity wasted in making up stories? In an earlier chapter, I agreed with Freud's assessment that dreams were the guardians of sleep, that maintaining the dreamer's interest in dream content, he becomes reluctant to leave the dream theater by waking up. The more intelligent, and, consequently, the more creative dreamer requires a more interesting plot than a wittle wed wabbit wunning to prevent him from leaving the dream theater because of unendurable boredom. In addition, the creativity practiced in dreams may hone that gift for daytime use, a secondary utility of dreaming.

Many dream analysts believe that the dream state allows the unconscious mind to operate in an unfettered way, allowing it to solve problems of the waking state. They give the classical example of Kekule's (Fredrich Kekule (1821-1896) dream that solved the chemical structure of benzene. Apparently, he was unable to determine the molecular configuration of benzene, slept on it and had a very simple dream of six snakes joined from head to tail in a hexagonal "ring". As I indicated earlier, the royal road between dreams and the unconscious is a two-way street. So, we wonder if the dream led to the solution, or did the solution, already worked out unconsciously, led to the dream.

Another example is the famous *Bovine Dream* of Einstein. It is a lengthy, complicated dream, which he may have discussed with Freud. Although it occurred in his teens, it was well remembered into his adult life and seemed to haunt him for many years. Supposedly, it was that dream that led to his *Special Theory of Relativity* which included: the constant speed of light, simultaneity, the stretching of time and the demolition of the concept of absolute time. It is difficult to articulate a well-structured version of the dream, but what I can briefly state is that it involved the reaction of grazing cows to an electrified fence as observed by a farmer and Einstein himself. I mention the dream here only to illustrate, as in the Kekule/benzene case, the possible mechanisms for problem solving in dreams. In the case of the *Bovine Dream*, did Einstein, as a teenager, solve the problem of absolute versus relative time and then make it into a dream or, haunted by the dream for ten years, was he able to solve the absolute/relative problem which he then offered to the world at age twenty six in 1905 in his revolutionary *Theory of Special Relativity*?

The benzene and the bovine dreams may be myths, just as Galileo's Leaning Tower of Pisa story and Newton's getting hit on the head with an apple story. Kekule's dream and Einstein's dream may never have happened, but I like them as much as the Pisa and apple stories. Somehow, I find them inspirational and hope that science teachers would not stop telling them.

I have never had the good fortune of experiencing problem solving in *remembered* dreams, but I don't deny that it could have occurred in *forgotten* dreams, dreams that were shifted into my unconscious, only to enhance my problem solving ability later on when awake and focusing on the unsolved problem.

The more creativity we put into a dream, the more complicated it becomes, and the more complicated the dream, the more it sparks our interest. We have more desire, interest and prompts in complicated dreams, and, as a result, they are more likely to be remembered. Nothing improves our memory more than when we consciously exercise it. Dreams can be simple, complicated or in between depending on the concentrations of neurotransmitters that control the gates to memories. In my experience, there are factors that modify the concentrations of neurotransmitters in dreams, they include what we eat and body temperature.

Directly or indirectly, the food we eat supplies us with neurotransmitters. Patients with Parkinson's disease are encouraged to eat fava beans which are rich in dopamine, the neurotransmitter that is in short supply in a certain area of the brain associated with movement. I know through my own experience, and I have frequently heard it said by others, that the meal they had last night (especially if prepared by an amateur chef) made the weirdest dreams. Eating a lot of neurotransmitters, if they cross the blood brain barrier, will increase their concentrations in the brain, opening the gates to more memory neurons, resulting in very complicated dreams.

In high school chemistry lab we learned that applying heat frequently hastens chemical reactions because atoms and molecules move faster and bump into one another more often because of the energy imparted to them by heat. Most of us have experienced our wildest dreams when we were ill with fever, which, most likely, was associated with accelerated neurochemical reactions energizing neurotransmitters to open more gates. In children especially, fevers frequently induce hallucinations, "Mommy, get that elephant out of my room". This can also happen in certain vulnerable adults, who have never shown even the slightest trace of psychosis, and it is called "delirium". As with most dreams, such an experience is quickly forgotten. Many people experience delirium when they are about to die, not because it is a harbinger of death but because it is an indication of a vital organ failure that effects the brain. Frequently, the organ failure can be corrected, the delirium remits, and the patient survives. An elderly gentleman who I had seen in consultation for delirium secondary to pneumonia, threatened to report me to the Ethics Committee of the local medical society when I sent him a bill for my services. He not only denied ever seeing me but that he had ever been in the hospital suffering from delirium.

When we get into bed and close our eyes, our goal is to fall asleep. The time required to do so is variable, depending on fatigue, worries about the future, the many thoughts of remote and recent events and the planning of survival strategies for the next day. Those thoughts are periodically interrupted by memories arising from the unconscious over which we have no control; eventually, all of the memories while falling asleep become involuntary. Then we enter deep sleep, a state of unawareness of our existence, which, retrospectively, we enjoy. (How could that be?) After an interlude of that kind of enjoyable death experience, we find ourselves suddenly resurrected in a dream. Thinking of recent and remote events, as we are falling asleep, opens specific memory gates, and as a result, our dreams contain both recent and remote but not necessarily related memories. Frequently, both the recent and remote memories have entropied with time.

Recently, I have noticed that, when I take a daytime nap, I immediately get into a dream without going through the deep sleep stages, as we normally do at night. The quality of these dreams seems to be somewhat different in that they exhibit less creativity in their story telling than regular night time dreams. I would say they are less dramatic and less interesting.

With the end of a dream, we might gradually enter the fully awake state. Not infrequently, as we are on our way to full wakefulness, we will dump the telepathic communication of dreams in favor of the vocal communication that we use in the waking state, even though we are not fully out of the dream. Although we are not aware of the change, our bed partner will frequently bring it to our attention at the breakfast table the next morning.

When we want to stay in the dream either because it is pleasurable or we are curious or want to fix it in our memory we should lie very still and concentrate on the dream content. Movement makes the dream and memory of its content go away more rapidly. This technique works for a brief period of time, but as we all know, no matter how hard we try, amnesia will, most likely, win out.

In order to understand the incorporation of events into dream content, it is necessary to be aware of some biographical data of the dreamer. After all, short term, long term, important and trivial memorable experiences have their role in determining dream content. Where do they lead? In this case, to my dream of March 7, 2009.

These are some of the memories that my unconscious, creative mind used to construct that dream, which I recalled *after* the dream:

For two days prior to my dream, I was experiencing intermittent right lower abdominal pain with some nausea. Having had numerous attacks of renal colic in the past, that was my first and best diagnosis, even though my urine had not yet turned into tea. My first attack was twenty seven years earlier when, on the way home from a day trip to northern Connecticut, I became very ill with flank and abdominal pain, nausea and vomiting and bloody urine. As a physician I knew that I was experiencing the symptoms of a kidney stone, and if it was two millimeters or less, I would pass it. Martha and I decided that we would stop at the first motel that we encountered. It turned out to be a seedy one. Having urinated many times, I finally heard that blessed, unforgettable, high pitched tinkle of the stone striking the porcelain of the toilet signaling that my suffering was, at least, temporarily over.

Ever since I enjoyed the horror movie, *Hell Motel* (the *o* is missing because that part of the neon is not working. It should read Hello Motel), where guests arriving at the motel were bound, had their vocal cords slit so they were mute and buried up to their necks in the proprietor's "garden", later to be harvested, dismembered with sharp instruments and sold as gourmet sausage or grade A prime at the adjoining grocery and meat market, I have been fearful of spending the night in motels. And of course, the Bates motel in *Psycho* reinforced my motel phobia.

More biography: For about two months prior to the dream, Martha had been experiencing an agonizingly painful foot problem causing a noticeable limp. On the day of my dream I received an invitation in the mail from St. Vincent's Medical Center for active staff members and their families to attend "The Family Fun Day" on Sunday March 31. This brought to mind the last St. Vincent's affair for benefactors of the hospital that we attended several months earlier. It was an extremely enjoyable affair with extraordinary hors d'oeuvres. It was well attended. In fact, the place was packed with the well to do major benefactors of the Medical Center and others who gave generously of their time and effort to promote the mission of the hospital. As one would expect, the women were bejeweled and flawlessly coiffured. Some of the men wore tuxedos. A very snazzy affair. Somehow, Martha and I became separated, and we began looking for one another. At one point I thought I saw her but was mistaken. Panic was about to set in when I saw Martha at a distance. She was wandering about looking lost. I raised my hand to get her attention with instant success. Reunited, we enjoyed the rest of the evening immensely.

Over the years, I have had my doubts about group therapy. I am sure it is helpful for certain select patients with specific psychiatric diagnoses. What I see now, is it being used to treat almost all psychiatric diagnostic categories –

one treatment fits all. But even in the unselected cases, I concede that there are benefits derived from the socialization in therapy groups. They frequently break through the social isolation that is so common in psychiatric patients who may carry a great variety of diagnoses. What I am saying is that group therapy is not enough.

On the day of the dream, I watched a fair amount of television. There was a news story about a group of irate individuals who were duped into investing with Bernie Madoff, of Ponzi scheme fame, and lost their hard earned fortunes. There was a report on poor, young Asian girls kidnapped and forced into prostitution and slavery by unscrupulous entrepreneurs. There was a documentary on the History channel that suggested an immense conspiracy that included the military, the FBI and CIA, the purpose of which was to withhold the reality of alien visitations from outer space. On another channel I saw the commercial with the terminal message, "What happens in Vegas stays in Vegas". I wondered why someone would advertise with pride a conspiracy of silence.

When I took the flag in that evening, I noticed the paint on the pole was peeling.

The dream: Martha and I were driving down a country road. We decide to check in at a motel for the night. We settle in, and suddenly I found Martha missing. I searched the vicinity without success, and in a panic, I reported her absence to the manager who appeared very concerned and called the police. A plain clothes policeman immediately appeared on the scene. He was reassuring of a favorable outcome. He began his investigation with the help of three or four others, including a female psychologist and a private detective. All were very reassuring and urged me not to worry. Suddenly, I found myself at what was some kind of psychiatric institute, not a hospital but some kind of special place, an "institute" where the focus is on some sort of group therapy for the realization of one's potential for self-improvement. (I have always been skeptical of such "institutes" and their motivational speakers.) It then came to my mind that this team of investigators was imposters; they were actually involved in a widespread conspiracy to cover up Martha's disappearance. I was then in a wide corridor with doors. Desperate to find Martha, who I knew was hidden there, I started breaking down doors. Behind each door there was a group therapy in session with a therapist and "patients", all affluent, young (thirty to forty), very well dressed and pleased to be there but no Martha. Suddenly, the place turned into a large, hotel type special events room, resembling a gym, and there was gambling going on. I was still desperately searching for Martha. The people there looked the same as the people in the group therapies. I noticed that all the women had dark hair like Martha and her identical body-build. I knew it would be very difficult to find her. I decided to look for a woman with Martha's limp. Coming up empty handed and more desperate, I started attacking the women and pulling their hair. I felt that Martha was in the crowd, and others were disguised to look like her to make her presence difficult to detect. They were all conspirators in some evil plot. I pulled the dark hair of one woman, and it turned out to be a wig, hiding straw blond hair. Suddenly I had a flagpole in my hand and raised it to signal Martha that I was there to rescue her. No acknowledgment, I was sure that her lack of response had to do with a threat that I would be tortured and killed if she revealed her presence. (Martha has always been an overprotective wife, and although her over protectiveness assures me of her love and is always directed toward my survival, it is, at times, an annoyance, since I am frequently prohibited from doing things around the house that need to be done.) I then had the idea that if I could break the conspiracy of silence I would find her. I made the announcement in that crowded room that the management, because of the economic crisis, could no longer keep the promise it made regarding their retirement funds. In fact, there would be zero money for their retirements. 401Ks all gone, I hoped it would cause them to rebel against the top conspirators and reveal Martha. I then found myself at the bar. Aside from a few groans from the crowd, there was no sign of discontent. Another failure. "You know what's going on here don't you?" The question came from a slightly built, balding, sixtyish bartender with a generic face who I immediately felt I could trust to help. At first I thought it was my uncle Stanley, but it turned out to be the villainous proprietor of Hell Motel. Nevertheless, I felt confident that I would find her and began to plan our escape. I gave up the idea of calling the FBI for fear of ending up with more imposters. I planned that we both would be silent. The car would be bugged, and certainly, we couldn't go back to the motel where all our stuff was. End of dream. Now awake, I was overjoyed to find Martha lying safely beside me.

Recalling the recent and remote memories that I had enumerated prior to the narrative of my dream, I understood the construction of the dream's content. Memories of faces, places and events together with the innate creativity of the dreamer, produced a dream that was incoherent and crazy but certainly interesting and thought provoking to the dreamer. Magically, and without any effort, a two millimeter stone causing abdominal pain resulted in a complicated dream. Within one half hour after awakening from the dream, I was able to make the connections between the dream content and my recent and remote memories.

Now, after all that, I repeat, *dream content is unimportant*. We forget dreams because it is not important to remember them, even though it is important to have them. Once they are over, they have done their job and become useless clutter in the mind.

If you are in the mood for entertainment, let dream dissection entertain you without charge. You probably have been doing it automatically. In some way it is similar to dream analysis as previously described but has nothing to do with dream content as symbols; it is simply isolating the elements of the dream and connecting them to recent and remote memories. One becomes an expert after practicing on one or two dreams. As I have suggested before, when you wake, keep your eyes closed and don't move; this will help you to remember the dream content. Once you remember its content, try to make the connections to memories. Making the connections will further encode the dream content in your memory bank, and you may be able to enjoy the dream retrospectively, even the nightmares. However, despite your best effort to encode the dream in long-term memory, you will find it difficult to remember it even for a few hours. Your long term memory bank is reluctant to take your deposit. If, for some reason, you are intent on remembering it (like to please your Freudian dream analyst), you can try to write it down as soon as you awaken. I did that to write this chapter. When awake and exercising memory for real events, we find it easiest to remember that which is logical. When we awaken after dreaming and try to remember what we dreamed, we find it is easiest to remember what is illogical and incoherent.

A fairly common dream experience is to wake up, say, after four hours of sleep, from a dream for which you have a good memory, only to have the feeling that there was a part of it that went before but was forgotten. With some effort you may start to remember, but peculiarly, that part of the dream memory is totally disconnected. The coherence in place and time that one would expect in a single dream is lacking. What has happened here is that there were two dreams, the most recent one remembered well and without effort, while the one before required effort to bring it to consciousness. So that kind of lack of coherence is a clue to the presence of more than one dream. Such an experience makes dreaming even crazier than it is.

Freudian psychology holds that dream content, the what of dreams, reveals what is happening in the unconscious mind but fails to tell us why or how. Let's find out.

Chapter 6

WHAT'S THE USE?

"... Nature ... prefers to endow one thing with many effects"

N. Copernicus

On day zero God created Mother Nature, hired her as a nanny and charged her with the safety and well-being of all of His children, giving her a lot of authority. She made the rules and immediately made them strict, VERY strict, never to be broken, all in the interest of her brood. (God helped you if you broke them; that was called a miracle.) At times however, she doesn't let us know what the rules are and why they are so. With more than a little touch of arrogance she tells us, "That's for me to know and for you to find out". Just as you think you know the rules, she might change them. Then she claims that none of the rules have been changed, they were never changed, and it's our fault that we didn't read them carefully enough. How can she expect us to read something written in ten dimensions. She is incredibly inflexible, accepts no excuses. She is hard to live with but impossible to live without. She doesn't allow conjunctions in her vocabulary, no ifs, ands or buts. Nor does she accept

conditions, additions, subtractions, exceptions or substitu-
tions. It is her way, her way, her way. PERIOD!

As far as we know, it is true that the laws of nature
never change, but we have been their observers for a very
short time. Our knowledge of them certainly doesn't change
them, but it helps us to cooperate with them and them with
us for the benefit of mankind. For example, knowing the
gravitational constant has led to the exploration of space and
jobs, jobs, jobs.

Mother Nature's prodigious efforts are not just to assure
survival of God's favorite creation but also to make our
survival more comfortable and pleasant. The table at the end
of this chapter is a comparison of diverse naturally occurring
physical objects (vegetation, iron and moon) with the mental
(dream). Although there is a vast difference between what is
physical and what is mental, what they have in common are
primary and secondary utilities which are directed at the
survival of the individual and the species. Their tertiary utilities may also be directed at survival, but, generally, in our
current environment are directed toward comfort and pleasure. What immediately becomes obvious is that both the
physical and the mental are necessary for survival.

Our ancestors (Homo sapiens) of over 250,000 years or
even Homo habilis (the tool maker) of over two million
years ago were aware of the secondary and tertiary utilities
of vegetation, i.e., survival. They were unaware of its primary, i.e., photosynthesis. Nor did they know anything
about any of the utilities of iron or the Moon. Certainly, they
must have known that the primary utility of mental phenomena (the cognitive functions of thinking, perceiving and
remembering) also was survival. Although it was unlikely
that they were able to verbalize it, they knew it intuitively.

Being that thinking, perceiving and remembering are
important components of dreaming, it would seem that we
would have the same intuitive knowledge about the primary
utility of dreams as our ancestors had about the intuitive

connections between these cognitive functions and survival. I believe that we have avoided or denied that connection because dreams are crazy, and who of us would want to entrust a crazy with the responsibility for survival.

Whatever is has purpose. Purpose is the "why" of existence. Because Mother Nature is parsimonious, she endows things with multiple purposes; she will not produce something new for a purpose that can be achieved by something that already exists. Nature has produced things that always have primary and sometimes have secondary utilities. She refuses to get involved with tertiaries, that is left to man's creativity. The following criteria are suggested for primary, secondary and tertiary utilities:

Primary:

- They are necessary for survival.
- They are beneficial for and apply to all mankind.
- They are usually hidden from us but may be discovered by intense scientific investigation or logic.
- They show no evidence of the creativity of man.

Secondary:

- They are necessary for survival.
- They are not beneficial for nor do they apply to *all* mankind.
- They are usually not hidden from us.
- They show no evidence of the creativity of man.

Tertiary:

- They are occasionally necessary for survival.
- They are usually necessary for comfort or pleasure.
- They are not beneficial for nor do they apply to *all* mankind.
- They are not hidden from us.
- They *always* show evidence of the creativity of man.

A book has no primary or secondary utilities. It is produced by the voluntary effort of its author. It is the product of the creativity of man and serves the needs of a few and has nothing to do with survival – we can live without books. All of a book's utilities are tertiary and may include: a source of revenue for the author, the communication of ideas, burning it for heat or protest, a gift when you can't think of anything better to get for a friend's birthday. Carelessly left on the coffee table unread, it can also be used to impress one's guests with one's literacy and sophistication. None of these are primary or secondary utilities; they are all tertiaries because they are all the result of the voluntary creativity of man. While man's creativity and memory are used voluntarily when awake and involuntarily in dreams, the same memories and the same creativity are used whether we are awake or asleep and dreaming, an example of Nature's way of endowing one thing with more than one effect.

Adam and Eve believed that the purpose of trees was to provide apples. I am sure they never even suspected that their prime purpose, which wasn't discovered until the seventeenth century, was photosynthesis with its life sustaining oxygen. Consider here the plethora of secondary and tertiary utilities of trees: to supply nourishment (fruit), as a building material (lumber), as a source of heat (firewood), as a coolant (shade), to beautify one's property, as a gym that challenges little boys and girls to test their strength and coordination, as a safe nesting place for birds, as something scared cats can climb to escape the jaws of unfriendly dogs. I am sure the reader can add dozens more to this admittedly short list.

Iron is just one of the eighty-one of the naturally occurring (not synthetically prepared by a collider) elements supplied to this planet by the Prime Provider. The primary utility of iron, which together with nickel, forms the molten core of this planet, is to produce a shield, the magneto-sphere, that protects us from deadly cosmic radiation, a necessary preparation for the arrival and survival of life forms. Most of the time, it does its job well. Unfortunately, some of the bad rays, which are highly energetic protons, may break through the shield and smash into one of Mom or Dad's helixes (DNA), and produce an unwanted mutation in their offspring. To discover the secondary and tertiary utilities of iron, all one has to do is to look around. Whatever you see is either made of iron, contains iron or has been manufactured by various iron tools.

Although we have discovered secondary uses for many elements through their unique physical properties, i.e., crystalline structure, boiling and melting points, density, valence, atomic numbers and atomic weights, which we have learned through the use of the *Periodic Table of Elements*, we have no knowledge of the prime purpose of most of them. At the present time we do know the prime utility of elements C, O, H, Na, Cl, Fe, K, N and S; all are necessary for life.

To ascertain the primary utility of the Moon at this point is difficult. Three are in competition for first place: to expertly tug on Earth to produce the gradual seasonal changes necessary for the production of food crops, tidal changes necessary for some aquatic life forms and the protective function it has served over four billion years by taking many hits, especially on its dark side, from asteroids and meteors bound for Earth – it has spared us from numerous catastrophic collisions. Hopefully, it will continue to do its job of protecting us from those nasty asteroids that we are becoming increasingly concerned about.

Secondary uses include: as a calendar, giving farmers extra hours of light during the autumn harvest and as an astronomer's delight. (By far, the Moon is the most readily accessible and most interesting heavenly body for professional and amateur astronomers.)

It was used by Einstein as an ingenious tool as it occulted the Sun during the total eclipse of 1919 when, as a tertiary utility, it allowed the taking of certain photographs and measurements that proved the existence and curvature of the fabric of spacetime in the proximity of very massive objects like stars and planets. It confirmed his *Theory of General Relativity*. (Newton had theorized that there was something within massive objects that caused the gravitational force. Einstein believed that it was the "warping of the geometry of spacetime" that was responsible for gravity. Both theories accommodate nature's inverse square, discovered by Newton, that tells us how the universe is constructed.)

So, what does all that have to do with dreams? Dreams included in the theories of Freud or Jung or yours or mine are constructed according to nature's recipe, $D = mc^n$ that doesn't change no matter what the theory.

Most of us have long been acquainted with the secondary and tertiary utilities of trees, iron and the Moon. Few of us were ever even aware that they had primary utilities. It is the primary utilities that Mother Nature wants to keep secret. She will grudgingly reveal them to those who persistently nag her like Copernicus, Kepler, Galileo, Newton, Lemaitre, Curie, Watson, Crick, Darwin, Wallace, Mendel, Hoyle, Gell-Mann, Kandel and dozens of Nobelists and ordinary insomniacs who work tirelessly in the laboratories of their minds to discover the primaries while everyone else on the planet is asleep.

We have positive knowledge of things when we know what they are. We have negative knowledge when we know what they are not. Our knowledge frequently starts with the negative. For example, suppose we know nothing about a ball except that it is not green. That definitely adds to our knowledge about the ball but not much. We are able to add to this negative knowledge by continuing to eliminate all the colors that the ball is not, always increasing our knowledge. Finally, when all colors but red are eliminated, we come up with the positive knowledge that the ball is red, at which point all the negative knowledge becomes useless. Dreams offer no negative knowledge; they present only positive knowledge, but fortunately, (Yes, I said fortunately.) they offer only false positive knowledge, a pack of lies presented and experienced as the truth which is only discovered to be false when we awaken.

Already knowing since infancy that the laws of gravity do not permit us to fly without machine, a dream of flying adds nothing to our positive knowledge of gravitational attraction because it is false. A dream of bilocation adds nothing to our positive knowledge of the impossibility of being here and there at the same time because it is false. A dream of reversing the arrow of time into the past adds nothing to our positive knowledge of the passage of time because it is false. Dreams are useless in providing reliable positive or negative knowledge of reality.

Once these dream experiences are corrected when awake by our positive knowledge of reality, that we cannot fly, we cannot bilocate, we cannot change the arrow of time, all that dream stuff becomes close to useless. *For the most part, dream content is valueless junk.* Its only utility is the breaking of known physical laws that allow us to identify it as a dream when we awaken. Dream content has nothing to do with increasing our knowledge of anything. It is full of baloney. It tells us as much about complexes as it does about the future. In my experience, as far as I know for certain, it has not provided solutions to any of the problems of my waking life.

Tertiary utilities reveal the unmistakable fingerprints of man. As I have mentioned in the beginning, the only tertiary utility of dreams that I have been able to identify is its use to provide comfortable livings for dream analysts, fortunetellers and the like and people like myself who try to write books about them. As you already know, tertiary utilities serve a certain select segment of the population. In the case of dream analysis it is the wealthy, bored intelligentsia. Although dream analysis is of no therapeutic value, it has become a status symbol in some circles comparable to vanity license plates that people are willing to pay extra for to enhance their self-esteem.

Dreams are guardians of sleep, royal roads to the unconscious, enhancers of memory and creativity and nighttime entertainers, all of which have been discussed earlier. These are all secondary utilities. In addition, when there is the bringing together of recent and remote memories in a dream, there is the consolidation of the past and near present, resulting in a more unified feeling of who we are. It is very common in dreams to visualize ourselves at an earlier age because all memories are of past events when we were younger. They reinforce the idea that the person we are today is one and the same person we were many years ago. I have never had a dream of being older. (We can't have memories of future events.) I enjoy getting reconnected to my twenties and thirties when I was confident that I knew all there was to know about medicine, psychiatry and life in general. Let's call this secondary utility "unification of the dreamer".

Another secondary utility of dreams would be the acting out of our ego dystonic (unacceptable) sexual and aggressive drives. These drives become especially obvious in the sexual "wet dreams" of adolescent and young adult males and the dreams of violence directed at authority figures, those we love and those we hate. We can enjoy those dreams without fear of retaliation, although they may briefly result in feelings of guilt upon awakening.

It may appear that there is a contradiction here since I have repeated earlier that dream content is unimportant. Allow me to clarify by pointing out that *it matters not what the content is as long as there is content*. Any old content is useful in accomplishing the task of producing the primary, secondary and tertiary utilities of dreams.

UTILITIES	VEGETATION	IRON	MOON	DREAMS
PRIMARY	Photosynthesis, O_2	Magneto-sphere, protection against cosmic rays	Shield from asteroids	Awareness, protection against predators
SECONDARY	Food and nutrients	Hemo-globin, O_2	Seasonal and tidal tugging, extra light for harvest-ing	Guardians of sleep, royal road to the unconscious, unification of the dreamer, enhancement of memory and creativity, acting out sexual and aggressive impulses, night time entertainment
TERTIARY	Building material, firewood, paper, shade, beautification, nesting place	Everything is made of iron or iron tools used in their manu-facture	Astrono-mer's delight, Ein-stein's eclipse	Improved standard of living for psycho-analysts, fortune tellers, science writers and lucid dream instructors.

Table 6 A comparison of the primary, secondary and tertiary utilities of vegetation, iron, the moon and dreams. Note that all have the primary utility of survival, and all have the tertiary utility of human creativity. Also note that the secondary utilities of dreams are not necessary for survival but include all of mankind.

PART TWO

WHY WE GO THERE

Chapter 7

AWARENESS, THE PRIMARY UTILITY OF DREAMS

"Cogito, ergo sum"
R. Descartes

All who are conscious are aware. All who are aware are not necessarily conscious. Consciousness is the observed state of the subject made by an outside observer. Awareness is the personal experience of the subject which may occur when he is unconscious. A patient undergoing surgery under general anesthesia is observed as being unconscious, but his state of awareness is not observable. Many individuals have reported out of body experiences when they were unconscious. Many more have reported hearing conversations of the surgical staff when they were deeply anesthetized. In both situations of unconsciousness there is awareness. Surgeons and their assistants have learned to take great care of their conversations in the presence of anesthetized patients. In all stages of sleep we are unconscious, when we dream we are aware.

As the reader must suspect by now, there is nothing, *absolutely nothing*, more important to survival than awareness. That being so, we must assume that there are important connections between survival, awareness and dreams.

Frequently, it seems that Mother Nature has made all survival tools imperfect or inoperative. People starve, cosmic rays kill us, asteroids smash into our planet and the awareness associated dreaming has more failures than our high tech security systems in protecting us from predators. When those things happen, believe it or not, the rules she set down on day zero are being obeyed, although it seems at times, that she is breaking her own rules. If, as we frequently expect of good Mother Nature, obstacles to survival were eliminated, we would not even be able to comprehend the concept of death; life everlasting would be a physical reality rather than a religious belief. Obviously, Mom doesn't want us around all the time; she's afraid she can't handle all of us kids. She worries about planetary overpopulation. She doesn't want to appear unfair or inconsistent, so she applies the same rules fairly, even to the best of her charges – they all must die. But she does give her favorites more survival time. Some Darwinians called it the survival of the fittest, ignoring the fact that even the fittest, as individuals or as species, do not survive forever.

The main survival tool for man and the animals higher up on the evolutionary scale is the knowledge of their existence. This self-awareness probably exists in one special area of the brain which is yet to be determined. Specific functional areas of the brain are mapped out by experimentalists and are usually proven by ablation either accidental or induced. If the area of Broca, lying in the left inferior motor cortex, which has to do with motor speech, is ablated by stroke or injury, the individual so afflicted will be unable to articulate words. Most likely a similar, sub-cortical area exists in the brain which when damaged, produces a lack of awareness of one's self, that is, a lack of knowledge of one's existence. Peculiarly, non-brain-damaged humans experience lack of awareness of their existence on a regular basis. This occurs in *dreamless* sleep which deprives us of our main survival tool. We are then totally at the mercy of whatever predators are lurking about, waiting for that unguarded opportunity to catch us unaware.

We not only have the protective tool of self-awareness during our waking hours but also during *dream* sleep. The self-awareness in both of these situations is most likely determined by the same neurons since the knowledge of existence is no different in the waking or dream state. You either know you exist or you don't.

Will the experimentalists be able to map out the precise area in the brain responsible for self-awareness? In the non-dreaming sleep when the senses are inoperative, it is impossible for the subject to report lack of awareness of his existence. He is dead to the world. However, it seems to me, it would be a simple matter to find the area in the brain responsible for self-awareness by the placement of multiple electrodes and finding what area in the brain becomes electrically "silent" in dreamless sleep. Another possibility would be by visualizing its position by PET scanning during dreamless sleep.

Better yet, for those like myself, who have no access to these wonderful and expensive tools, I suggest, as I have done and encouraged my colleagues to do and encourage my readers to do, is to try to actually get the feeling of what part of the body is responsible for the awareness of existence. Obviously it will not be the extremities or the torso but the head and more specifically, the brain. Encouraging more specificity, it, by consensus, appears to be located not in the back of the brain or in the sides of the brain but centrally about five inches from the bridge of the nose which would bring it roughly to the hypothalamic area just above the pituitary gland. This seems to me to be a nicely protected position since it lies in the region of the third ventricle with all of its shock absorbing cerebral spinal fluid. To get the feeling for the location of the center for awareness may take a little practice but persevere. Furthermore, it seems logical that the area(s) where the awareness neurons reside would be bilateral and, most likely, lying in the lateral walls of the third ventricle, bilateral because of the importance of the awareness of existence. If the area on one side was destroyed by stroke, trauma or tumor, the corresponding area on the other side would remain functional.

Such an arrangement is suggested by the interesting neurological condition known as left-sided neglect. (Right-sided neglect also occurs but is far less common.) In this condition a lesion (stroke, tumor or injury) in the right parietal lobe, the area of the brain that mediates sensations of touch, pain and temperature from the opposite of the body, causes the unfortunate individual so afflicted to deny the existence of one side of his body. He may neglect to shave the left side of his face or deny that his left arm belongs to him. While he is aware that he exists, he is unaware of the obvious, that the left side of his face and his left arm are his. (Many of us have experienced, to a lesser extent, that same phenomenon when we have local anesthesia, say, for root canal. We have that illusion that half our face doesn't belong to us.)

If the lesion was bilateral, one might expect that there would be no awareness of existence in the waking state. How similar this would be to the biological machines described below, able to move but unable to appreciate their existence. On the other hand, self-awareness may simply depend on the number of functioning neurons in a species rather than on one specific location in the brain.

We safely assume that trees have no awareness of their existence. We have no compassion for them when they are mercilessly chopped or sawed despite their anthropomorphization by the poet who said, "… a tree who may in summer wear a nest of robins in her hair".

Shifting to the animal kingdom, we run into some formidable problems. It is a frequent occurrence in nature that the evolutionary process of some species will abruptly come to a halt. In many animals it came to a halt long before self-awareness arrived on the scene.

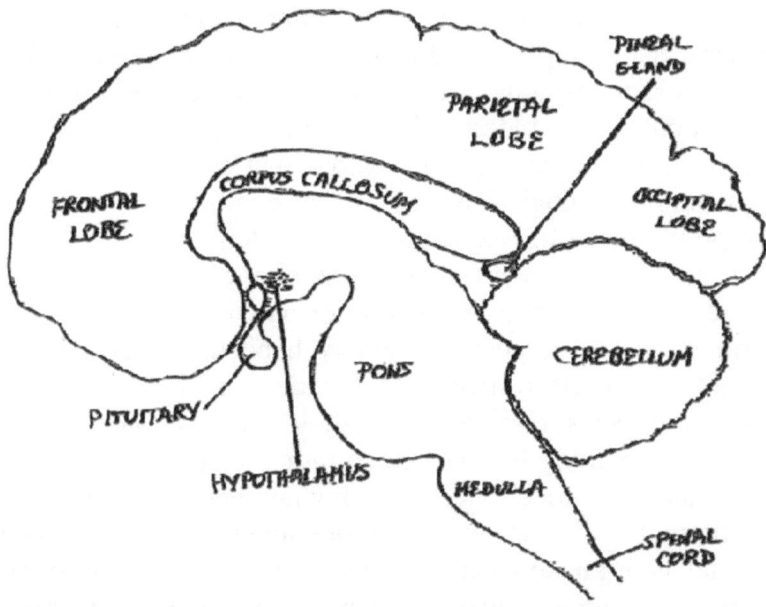

Figure 7 Medial surface of the right side of the brain, indicating the general area or seat of awareness of self. It is located in the hypothalamic area (stippled) above the pituitary gland.

At one extreme the protozoa are likely deprived of the knowledge that they exist. They are biological machines, robots, they may respond to light, heat, sound, vibrations and smells, but they have no awareness of their existence. They are like stones in that regard. Similarly, it is unlikely that invertebrates have an awareness of their existence so that if we step on a bug, by its squirming, it seems to be saying ouch, but it doesn't feel ouch. What we observe is simply bio-chemicals acting on a mangled biological structure. Just as one must experience awareness of existence to feel pain, one must experience awareness of existence to dream.

At the other extreme are the mammals which, together with man, have knowledge that they exist. I have no doubts that Fido and Pussy know that they are. In between bacteria and mammals is a large group of animals including insects, worms, fishes, reptiles and birds that we are not sure of. Do barnacles, clams, mussels, oysters, ants, mosquitoes, worms, bees, butterflies, spiders, flies, roaches and hundreds of yet undiscovered animal species know that they exist, or are they simply biological machines that exhibit all or some of the properties of life except for self-awareness?

Having spent a considerable number of hours searching for an indicator for the evolutionary beginning of self-awareness, I have come up empty handed. My best guess would be that self-awareness first made its evolutionary debut when a species reached a threshold of, say, one million neurons. Anything beyond one million would begin to result in complex non-mechanical, non-programmed behaviors. With continuing evolution, those neurons might have found their special, centralized location where they may be found today. With the passage of about four billion years, those neurons became surrounded by the numerous neurons specializing in the cognitive functions of thinking, perceiving and remembering and the executive functions such as attending, planning, organizing, sequencing, learning and problem solving and reasoning. From the humble beginnings of self-awareness we have arrived at Homo sapienship. Without such beginnings those biological machines would have remained biological machines like trees.

Our senses can be easily awakened by the morning Sun's strong rays penetrating our closed eyelids, by the not too gentle nudge from an irate bedmate to stop the intolerable snoring or by the loud fragrance of coffee, bacon and eggs ascending the stairs from the kitchen. Regrettably, the alcoholic lying in the roadway, who passed out after his "one for the road" and the surgical patient "etherized upon a table" appear to be deprived of all sensory experiences in their deeply anesthetized states and cannot be easily or uneasily awakened. They, from all outward appearances, are senseless, and if they die in this state they probably will not realize it until after they have served their time in purgatory.

Fortunately, for the alcoholic and the surgical patient and for us, while in dreamless sleep, the time in such a perilous state is self-limited; the alcohol and the ether are metabolized, and we exit out of dreamless sleep, all achieving a sensory state that lets us know once more that we exist and that we are alive and back on the track to survival. Thanks to this most necessary tool of awareness, we are able to preserve our lives at least minimally. The outside observer has correctly judged them to be unconscious, an objective state, while the drunk and the surgical patient may still be aware of their existence, a subjective state which I believe can exist without the functioning senses. This is the situation in which people in the persistent vegetative state find themselves; they have awareness of their existence, but they have no sensory experience and are unable to indicate their awareness of their existence. Fortunately, about fifty percent will recover; regrettably, life supporting measures are frequently prematurely withdrawn.

When we escape from that deadly, inanimate state of dreamless sleep by entering the world of dreams, we again summon up our most important defense for survival; we do that four or five times a night without even trying. The knowledge that we exist is totally absent in dreamless sleep (unlike in the persistent vegetative state) and unequivocally present in dream sleep, no matter if we are the actor, being acted upon or just a passive observer. Self-awareness is as essential a property of dreams as it is to waking life. It is that without which there can be no dream. During our waking activities, awareness and the accompanying alertness are the ultimate survival tools whether we are crossing a street, driving a car or a nail, sawing a board or attending a class or a meeting.

One may properly ask, if awareness is so necessary for survival why is it that we put ourselves in jeopardy by sleeping when predators are prowling about? On the one hand, it is obviously unsafe to sleep, while on the other hand, sleep itself is necessary for survival. It restores, by some chemical reaction, the energy necessary for the activities of daily living, including coping with threatening predators. Dreamless sleep supplies only energy, lots of energy. Dream sleep supplies both energy, although less than in dreamless sleep, and self-awareness, that important life-saving knowledge of existence. There may have been a time in evolutionary history when all sleep was dream sleep, considering those dangerous jungles in Africa crawling with carnivorous predators twenty-four seven. With the passage of a couple hundred millennia and with help of man's creativity and dreams, we have survived to our current level of civilization making it less and less necessary to spend so much time in dream sleep for survival. This allows for a greater amount of sleep time to be spent in the more energizing dreamless sleep. Dream sleep can be exhausting.

It would be interesting to measure the dream times of aboriginal people living in an equatorial jungle loaded with predators comparing them with the dream times of, say, the inhabitants of the wilds of New York City. The more dangerous the environment, the more dream sleep is required. With the advancement of hi-tech security, will dreams become unnecessary, atrophy and vanish?

Aside from day dreaming, which is an entirely different mental exercise, it is necessary for one to sleep in order to dream. It is difficult to determine at what point on the evolutionary scale that animals start to sleep. It seems certain to me that bacteria, amoebas and other nucleated unicellular animals do not sleep. Simple multicellular animals probably don't sleep; they are biological machines. However, being a biological machine does not guarantee around the clock wakefulness. Asian lady beetles, which I have observed for prolonged periods of time and which I regard as biological machines, sleep a great deal despite their lidless compound eyes that are always exposed to light. I am sure that other insects sleep even though they are biological machines. They sleep to restore and preserve energy, as we do, to do the tasks they were assigned to do by Mother Nature. As previously stated, sleep does not imply dreaming even in man, since dreamless sleep is universally experienced nightly. Some fish sleep in spite of their lack of eyelids and some don't, reptiles probably sleep and birds certainly sleep. All mammals sleep but remember, all sleepers are not necessarily dreamers.

Chapter 8

THE CRAZY MAKER

"A dream is a short lasting psychosis, a psychosis is a long lasting dream."

A. Schopenhauer

"A lunatic is a wakeful dreamer"

I. Kant

Early on, I had mentioned that all dreams MUST be crazy, and if they were not, we would be in deep trouble. The medical terminology for crazy is "psychosis". Psychosis is a pathological mental state characterized by delusions, hallucinations and bizarre behavior. A delusion is a false idea, e.g., "There is a conspiracy out there to kill me, or I am Jesus Christ in his second coming." A hallucination is a perception that occurs in the absence of an external stimulus. Common hallucinations include: hearing accusatory or commanding voices that others cannot hear, seeing visions that others cannot see, tasting non-existent poisons, smelling obnoxious odors and feeling worms under one's skin. None of which others can taste, smell or feel. As the result of delusions and hallucinations bizarre behavior can occur. The psychotic individual who is responding to his auditory hallucinations may be seen gesturing and talking to himself while standing in the middle of a busy thoroughfare, enraptured by a vision of God surrounded by His angels or screaming at strangers to stop following him and spying on him. These experiences are actually lies that the perceptive brain is telling to the believing mind and can be corrected with anti-psychotic medication but not by psychotherapy or psychoanalysis. Not only can these symptoms be corrected with medication but they can also be caused by medications and hallucinogenic drugs. Being that psychotic symptoms can be produced and relieved by drugs is an indication that these symptoms are due to the malfunction of the brain rather than of the mind; *matter in the form of drugs cannot interact with that which is not matter*. Obviously however, the symptoms are mental. Psychotic symptoms indicate the presence of *brain* pathology. It is unfortunate that psychoses are referred to as mental disorders since they are physical disorders of the brain.

Dreams have more clarity than the hallucinations of the psychotic. Psychotics will frequently ask a bystander to verify their false perceptions, while this does not seem to occur in dreams. The psychosis of dreams includes delusions, hallucinations and bizarre behavior, but is not caused by any brain pathology.

If the psychosis of dreams is not produced by any brain pathology, then how does it happen? Remember that our unconscious mind has a file filled with old and new memories and has access to a boundless amount of creativity. He does it in collusion with our senses to tell the big lies that we experience in our dreams. Although we know from a very early age that he is a pathological liar, we continue to listen to his lies several times a night. One would think he would put our memories to good use instead of using them to lie. But maybe lying is a good use.

The dream liar is never detected during the dream; he is very clever that way. It is only when the dream is over and he has escaped that we become aware of that scoundrel. The dream liar is not just a liar; he is also a law breaker. He breaks mathematical, physical, chemical, biological, psychological, philosophical, theological, moral and civil laws. He is a bad boy. Yet, Mother Nature allows him to practice his mischief. She allows him to do it four or five times a night for five to twenty minutes at a time. She even lets him get away with murder. Let me mention just a few of the perpetrations, many of which the reader will identify with, having witnessed them first hand on many occasions: The laws of mathematics are broken when $1 = 2$, that is, when the individual dreamer is seen as the actor in the dream by himself as the viewer (autoscopy) or when $2 = 1$, that is, when your wife and your mother are one and the same person. The laws of physics are broken when the laws of gravity are ignored and we fly without the aid of machine, or when we experience time travel into the past with reversal of the aging process; when we travel at the speed of light (at this point that technology is unavailable), allowing one to be in bed then instantaneously in Bejing. The laws of chemistry are broken when feces to turn into gold and vice versa. (Ah, Freud again.) The laws of biology are broken when in the dream, a person known to be dead is alive. The laws of psychology are broken when there is telepathic rather than verbal communication. Social and cultural laws are broken when we accept our Nobel Prize in the nude. In dreams, the laws of philosophy, including logic, epistemology, ontology, teleology and cosmology are broken en mass.

All this law breaking is perpetrated by the unconscious mind which is psychopathic and unrestrained by conscience. Dreams in which the dreamer is the actor engaged in moral and civil law breaking such as infidelity, incest, murder, rape, robbery, speeding, illegal parking, etc. may not be completely devoid of conscience. Consequently, there are a few individuals who feel guilty about what they dream and may require psychotherapy to relieve guiltless guilt. Generally, dreams have the unique utility of releasing repressed sexual and aggressive drives without restraint or accountability.

Dream psychosis can't be cured with medication; and I am sure that Mother Nature doesn't want it to be cured. She wants it to persist but intermittently; she gives some respite with periods of dreamless sleep. When we awaken, if we remember the dream, our conscious logical mind becomes aware of the lie and corrects it. All that stuff didn't happen – it was only a dream.

In dreams there is no continuity of time, space or mind; things just pop into and out of existence like the synthetically prepared elements of accelerators and colliders. How do we know if what we experienced in a dream was a lie or true? Law breaking is the clue. Most important would be the violation of physical laws as we know them. We experience "crazy physics" in dreams. One of the most important features of classical physics is that knowing the mass, position and velocity of a particle we are able to predict its future. In dreams, no matter how hard we try, we cannot predict where they will take us. Dreams are full of pop-ups. In real life, when we walk from one room to another, we can break down our movement into a series of steps, leading to our destination. In dreams, we frequently start at point "A" and pop-up at point "Z" without any appropriate intervening period of time or space, and unamazed, we experience it as real – Amazing.

Why has nature endowed us with such nighttime madness? Sometimes the best way to determine the usefulness of an object is to think it out of existence and analyze the consequences. In the case of Erwin's "dream" he has dreamed craziness out of existence, leaving him with a non-crazy "dream". See what can happen:

Erwin is seventy years old and a gentleman in every sense of the word. He was the owner of a small hardware store until it went under three years ago, being unable to compete with Home Depot's arrival on the scene. His wife died of cancer two years ago, and he has been living alone with his terrier mix, Pal, who was given to him by his daughter in the midst of his bereavement. Pal was therapeutic and did what psychiatrists with their best talking therapies and anti-depressants failed to do.

Erwin has had a very bad day. Earlier that evening he found a very dead Pal in a pool of bloody vomit that had the distinctive yellow streaking of Prestone. He is unable to sleep. The time projected on his bedroom ceiling is 1:30 A.M. He has not slept a wink. He was enraged. He knew who did it. He ruminated about the years of living next door to Mrs. Katz. By her name, he knew she was a dog hater.

She lived in that house with her parents since birth until they died forty years ago. She lived there for many years before Erwin and his family moved next door. She was an only child and spoiled rotten. By her late teens, nine out of ten board certified psychiatrists would have diagnosed her as having a rotten personality disorder. After she graduated high school, she was unable to hold down a job because of her personality traits. She had been living off her fairly nice inheritance until her present age of eighty five. She had been married briefly and had a daughter, Shirley, who left to get away from her as soon as she could, relocating in Maine. Although there was little love between them, Shirley duti-fully made sure that her mother had the necessities of food, clothing, shelter and medical care. She even gave Erwin a key to her mother's house and, despite his protests, paid him a small amount so that he would look in on her regularly to make sure she was all right.

The old lady's husband left the scene very suddenly many years ago, never to be heard from again. Now Erwin begins to suspect that Katz had done Sam in with Prestone, as she did with Pal, dismembered his body and planted the parts in her back door garden, which resembled a burial plot in size. He imagined that she poisoned Pal because he had been occasionally caught digging in her garden where he might uncover Sam's bones. She had regularly complained about Pal's doggy behavior in a shrill, threatening voice.

Erwin becomes even more enraged as he recalls the many kindnesses and favors he had done for Katz over the years: plunging her blocked toilet, shoveling her snow, cleaning her gutters, taking her shopping, driving her to medical appointments, rewarded only with criticism and never a word of gratitude or appreciation.

The time now projected on the ceiling is now 2:30 A.M. His rage increasing by the second, Erwin finds himself putting on his clothes. He comes downstairs and pauses indecisively at the back door. Stepping out, he starts counting 1-2-3-4-5-6........17-18-19-20........43-44-45........69-70-71..... 81-82-83-84-85-86-87. He was a compulsive counter and counted his steps from his back door to Katz's back door hundreds of times over the years, always eighty seven. He opens the door with his key and enters the darkened house. Silently, he walks up the stairs and enters Katz's bedroom. He quickly snatches the pillow from under her head and applies it with resolute pressure to her face. There was not even a weak struggle. He quickly replaces the pillow and leaves, going through his door to door counting ritual once again, eighty seven as usual. Now back at home, he goes into his bedroom, takes off his clothes and climbs into bed. The time is now 2:50 A.M. Sleep continues to be elusive. Suddenly, he is sitting upright in bed, sweating profusely and too scared to move. "WOW, what a dream! That was a dream wasn't it? How could I do something like that even in a dream? Is she alive or dead?" Deprived of logic, he wondered if she could be alive and dead at the same time. Feeling insanity rapidly approaching, he makes an unsuccessful effort to put it to rest for the night and to check on her the first thing in the morning. He literally counted forty winks, then gave up trying. Time passed slowly.

At 8:15 A.M. frantic knocking at the back door alerted him. It was Ruby, Katz's home health care aid. "Mr. Erwin,

Mr. Erwin, she's dead, she's dead!" He didn't have to ask her who, when or where. She had been suffering with coronary artery disease with congestive heart failure and shortness of breath for years. That was exactly what the medical examiner signed off on as the cause of death, with no suspicion of pillow suffocation.

Did he do it or didn't he? Unfortunately, Erwin's experience was a craziless one. If there was even the slightest hint of law breaking aside from the "murder". If only his step count was other than eighty seven, that would be a clue that it was only a dream, and he wasn't a murderer. He will never know what did or didn't happen because he was deprived of that which is most necessary for us to distinguish dream from reality, namely, the crazy physical law breaking. Craziness in dreams is *essential* and, fortunately, untreatable. Little wonder that Mother Nature puts up with that law breaking, lying unconscious mind.

Not infrequently, psychotic and demented individuals relate complicated dreams with obvious law breaking and are still unable to identify them as dreams. On one occasion, less dramatic than Erwin's fictional tale, I myself was unable to distinguish dream from reality: Unable to sleep, I got out of bed to look something up in a book. (Suffering from insomnia, I had done that many times in the past.) It was very simple and totally devoid of law breaking. I got up out of bed, took a few steps to where the book was on my dresser, quickly looked up what I wanted to, got back into bed and promptly fell asleep. The next morning I didn't, and to this very day, I don't know if it really happened or if I dreamt it. I believe that whenever we have a dream, without any apparent or remembered law breaking, that starts and ends with us in bed, it will yield the kind of dilemma that Erwin and I have experienced.

Fortunately, this is an infrequent occurrence. More frequently what happens is that, say, a spouse awakens in the morning irritable and angry because he or she has had a dream that the other was guilty of infidelity. It was as if there was an inability to distinguish dream from reality. Such a mood may last for minutes, hours or days and will remit spontaneously. On two or three occasions, I have treated patients with borderline personality disorder who, for years, were unable to let go of the anger precipitated by such a dream.

Chapter 9

LIFE AND DEATH

"To be or not to be"
Hamlet

We learn a lot through similes, metaphors and analogies. As teachers and learners we use these tools several times a day. In teaching we use them to describe, in learning we use them to understand. They are comparisons of what we know to what we don't know. They quickly enhance our ability to grasp elusive concepts more easily. We learn to use them automatically at a very early age.

Sleep is like death. Dreamless-sleep is like non-existence. Dream-sleep is like life after death in a place where natural laws no longer apply. Shakespeare's most famous six words are an indication that he has given life and death considerable thought, as we all have. We all are aware of the similarity between death and sleep, and most of us are mindful of the more accurate similarity between death and dreamless-sleep. The more religious and pessimistic among us, like Hamlet, are more frightened of death being like dream-sleep with the possibility of it being nightmarish. Right from the beginning it seems that Homo sapiens held the belief in a life after life and, like Hamlet, not knowing what that would be like, feared it. Those among us who are most narcissistic are more fearful of no life after life, a permanent dreamless-sleep, depriving the universe of our magnificent selves. At times we have the fear of non-existence of the narcissist and at other times we have the fear of life after life as spoken by Hamlet.

From time to time we become aware of and amused by paradoxes. Of interest to me in this work is the absurdity of the fear of and the pursuit of death. In reviewing my life, I notice that there has been an ongoing desire to accelerate the arrow of time. Why was time moving so slowly? As a four year old I couldn't wait to go to school like my sister. Then it was the same with Christmas, my birthday, summer vacation, the carnival rides, the two-wheeler and all that other kid stuff. There was that prolonged painful waiting in childhood for good things to happen. I remember it well. It is very easy to understand the impatience of childhood considering the snail-like passage of time, which we experience much slower in childhood than in adulthood and much slower in adulthood than in old age. The older we get, the faster we seem to speed through life.

Strangely, even as adults with knowledge of the connection between the passage of time and death, that desire for temporal acceleration continues. We can't wait to complete our education, to get married, to reproduce, to see the kids grow up, to get the grandchildren civilized, to retire, to die and get out of purgatory fast. Then there are the numerous trivial things from getting the water to boil to finding out who our next president will be. We seem to prefer the future to the present. Hurry up death, hurry, come on, we can't wait! No, we don't want that. In fact, we are deathly afraid of it, yet wishing for the more rapid passage of time, a paradox. On the other hand, oddly enough, at the same time, we wish to decelerate and reverse the arrow of time through our treasured memories during the day and our dreams at night, a double paradox.

At the end of the day, exhausted by the ongoing pursuit of solutions to our never ending problems of daily living, we eagerly embrace dreamless-sleep, during which we have no more knowledge of our existence than a tree or a stone. We not only have no knowledge of our existence, but we have no knowledge of anything. None of our cognitive functions are operative. We savor that taste of death but only a taste.

If Descartes proof of existence is, "Cogito ergo sum" (I think therefore I am), then the corollary would be non-cogito ergo non-sum (I do not think therefore I am not.) A jury, impressed by the brilliance of Descartes and the logical argument of a defense attorney might acquit a defendant who murdered his victim who was in dreamless sleep. Of course that lawyer who used the non-sum defense would have to prove that the victim was in dreamless-sleep as opposed to dream-sleep when he would be cogitoing. (That could be done by first attaching an EEG machine to the victim that showed stage three or four sleep at the time of the murder.) To kill the dreamless-sleeper or the passed out drunk or the anesthetized patient or the unconscious acci-dent victim is illegal even though, just as a stone, they are not aware of their existence. What makes it a crime is the victim's ability to regain such awareness when they dream or awaken; it is a crime when the non-awareness is not a permanent condition.

It is not illegal to "kill" a brain dead individual by "pulling the plug". Barring a miracle (as in the case of the biblical Lazarus), it is highly unlikely that such an individ-ual has any knowledge of his existence or ever will except in life after life. As previously mentioned the brain dead condi-tion should not be confused with the persistent vegetative state or the permanent vegetative state, both of which may be reversible.

Considering the above, and not knowing when embryo, fetus or baby in the womb achieve knowledge of their existence, as members of species Homo sapiens we should be concerned that this human life which, predictably, *will* have knowledge of its existence, is being legally terminated by the abortionist's curette. Should it not be afforded the same right to future self-awareness as the dreamless-sleeper, the passed-out drunk or the anesthetized surgical patient? Many will deny that what is aborted is human life. Even before the indisputable proof by DNA, it had been known for ages that the product of human conception would always be another human and never any other species, not even a hominid cousin. As far as what is aborted being life, it is obvious that if it were not living there would be no need for an abortion. Biology tells us that that thing is living; genetics tells us that it is human and uniquely individual; EEG machines tell us that REM sleep occurs even in utero, indicating dreaming or, at least and more likely awareness of existence.

The logic of the abortionist that justifies his craft is that the embryo, fetus and even the about to be born or partially born baby do not mind being aborted just as a stone doesn't mind being crushed into gravel – they don't cry, do they?

Aside from dreamless-sleep, there are the above mentioned states of non-awareness of existence in humans, all of which we hope to avoid. That non-existence sleep is so terrific and refreshing and we crave it so, but we don't want it to be permanent. In fact, we frequently fear that it might be and resist it.

How can it be that we crave the temporary non-existence of dreamless-sleep and dread the arguably permanent non-existence of death? Shakespeare analogizes sleep to death. Hamlet considers killing himself to achieve the trouble-free, dreamless sleep of non-existence. However, the thought comes to him that the sleep he seeks may not be dreamless, but may end up in dream-sleep with a dream far more unpleasant than his waking life existence, a nightmare.

Occasionally, I think how nice it would be to get a full eight hours of dreamless-sleep rather than having it interrupted periodically by dreams that may be unpleasant if not night-marish, sapping a good deal of my mental energy. I would have more energy the next day to do a better job, or would I? Probably not. Excessive energy leads to hyperactivity, sometimes agitation, euphoria, dysphoria, delusions and even hallucinations. It is what mental health professionals call "mania".

Mother Nature appears to be capricious or at least inde-cisive and sometimes senile. After all, she has been around an uncountable number of years. She toys with our aware-ness of existence. She allows us to be during our waking hours and dream-sleep and demands us not to be during dreamless-sleep. She seems to control these variations in awareness with a device similar to a thermostat. When we achieve a good amount of energy during dreamless sleep, which wastes no energy (not even the energy necessary to make us aware of our existence), she finds it necessary to switch us to the less energy efficient sleep mode of dream-ing which appears to be a mode of wasting energy on crazi-ness. A thermostat automatically calls up heat energy and when a specific temperature is reached, it shuts down pro-duction until the temperature falls to a predetermined level. Suppose it failed to turn off automatically. That nice, com-fortable thermal energy would increase to the point of hyperthermia, extreme discomfort and even death. If the energy that we accumulate during dreamless-sleep becomes excessive, we will wake up, and we will not be able to fall back to sleep until some of that excessive energy is used up, usually by worry of not being able to fall back to sleep or by some nagging problem of daily living. Thermostats prevent heat catastrophes. Sleep thermostats, "dreamostats", prevent such catastrophes from happening by shifting into the dream mode which requires the expenditure of excessive sleep energy, allowing sleep to continue. "Dreams are the guardians of sleep."

Suppose on the other hand, that the "dreamostat" failed to turn off dream-sleep and we spent all of our sleep time in dreaming. Would we waken depleted of energy, depressed instead of refreshed and unable to accomplish the activities of daily living, or would we awaken in a psychotic state as the result of an overflow of dream craziness into the waking state? Maybe Mother Nature is not ready for the nursing home. She may know what she is doing after all.

Chapter 10

SURVIVAL FROM BIG BANG TO DREAMER

"Man still bears in his bodily frame the indelible stamp of his lowly origin."

C. Darwin (1809-1882)

Out of nowhere, since there was no "where", an infinitesimal bundle of infinite energy appeared somewhere and exploded silently into what we now paradoxically call "The Big Bang". Fred Hoyle (1915-2001), who had a way with words, derisively named that event which Georges Lemaitre (1894-1966) theorized as the beginning of everything. Cosmologists have estimated the size of that bundle to be as large as a pea or as small as a proton. Lemaitre called it the "primeval atom". Since that moment 13.7 billion years ago when we all were born (when everything was born) as charged subatomic particles, we have experienced and survived unimaginable perils. (Because great men and great events are memorialized by the annual celebrations of their birthdays, it would seem appropriate that we should have an annual celebration, a universal Big Bang Day; not as the name would imply as something very noisy but as it really was, completely silent.)

108

Some Darwinians claim that we, the fittest, survived by unplanned evolution (just being at the right place at the right time), intelligent designists claim that we survived by design. However, how we got here is unimportant. The debate between the two has masqueraded as a scientific debate although, in reality, it is theological. The atheist evolutionists look at the grandeur and complexity of the universe and cannot imagine the existence of a being capable of creating it. The deistic evolutionists (intelligent designists), looking at the same universe, cannot imagine it as creating itself accidentally or by chance, undesigned. The debate boils down to whether the energy of Lemaitre's primeval atom was designed energy, (i.e., with a goal) or undesigned. Einstein tells us it was designed to produce mass times the speed of light squared, $E = mc^2$, (not $E = m^2c$ or mc^3). Crick, Watson and Wilkins tell us that their replicating double (not triple) helix is designed to be the building blocks of all life forms. Darwin, who claimed to be an agnostic but hinted that he might be an intelligent designist, tells us that his natural selection (survival of the fittest) is the design for the evolutionary progression of eukarya to the human frame. So far no one has been able to explain the design for the evolution of the mind. Both sides proselytize, but few minds are changed. The important thing is that we all have survived as the products of these designs.

Hard working scientists have discovered four "miracles". They didn't invent them and can't explain them, but they try. Although they insist that there are no such things as miracles, they haven't been able to account for them in any other way. No matter where we stand in the theological debate, we must be impressed by the inscrutability of:

1. The Big Bang. Energy being converted into matter resulting in our universe (Einstein's $E= mc^2$).

2. Matter being converted into life (replicating double helix of Crick, Watson and Wilkins).

3. Simple life forms evolving into extremely complex ones (Darwin's and Wallace's eukarya into hominids).

4. A chunk of complex living matter, represented by a special hominid, which we call the "missing link", achieving the ultimate "miracle", Homo sapiens.

Those brilliant men did not design their equations or formulas but discovered them.

Darwin's selection for the title of his revolutionary, evolutionary book, *The Descent of Man*, is puzzling. The general usage of "descent" implies movement from a higher level to a lower one. A book on evolution which has as its basic premise natural selection (the survival of the fittest) would be more appropriately entitled *The Ascent of Man*, which implies that, with time, man has been raised by natural selection from a less than human level to what he is now. The title is a contradiction to the basic proposition of his theory. What was he thinking? Remnants of Freudian doctrine make me suspect that Darwin experienced a Freudian slip of the pen that never was corrected. Freud may have wondered what was behind that slip. Perhaps that Darwin had doubts about his theory. (He "shuddered" at the idea of the evolution of the human eye, the anatomy and physiology of which he found to be so complex that he couldn't comfortably conform it to his theory.) "Descent" is more appropriate to devolution than to evolution. Did Darwin unconsciously believe that God created man in a superior state "in His likeness", who would devolve after "the fall" into the far from idyllic being we see now? Freud may have interpreted Darwin's conflict as a paradise lost/paradise yet to come complex, devolution vs. evolution.

Figure 10, Art vs. Science is composed of two panels representing the artist's and the scientist's version of the "adamization" of the missing link. 10-1 is Michelangelo's illustration, *The Creation of Man*. It is one of the many panels with which he decorated the ceiling of the Sistine Chapel. The missing link is portrayed in a reclining position with his arm and index finger extended, reaching out toward the extended arm and index finger of God. The fingers are not touching, so we don't know if the "adamization" had already taken place or was about to take place. The link is as handsome as any Hollywood movie star and even more handsome than David. He is well muscled and seems to be resting after coming home from his hair dresser and gym, where he did two hours on a Bowflex followed by an invigorating massage. If he speaks it would be in fluent Ciceronian Latin. He may have dabbed on some Aqua Velva for this special event. He is to be a made man, and as such he is entitled to special protection. He is not to be disrespected. He is to become a dreamer. The artist was obviously ignorant of the fact that we are all out of Africa, that Adam and Eve were black (if they weren't they wouldn't have survived, and we wouldn't be here), and there were possibly or even probably more than one Adam and Eve. (Nature is replete with back-ups.) Michelangelo has portrayed God as his usual anthropomorphic self with flowing white hair and beard. He looks ninety something, but, as we all know, He is considerably older; He hides his age well. For the majority of us, it is the only sensible way to grasp that elusive Concept.

10-1 The Creation of Man

ART
vs.
SCIENCE

10-2 The Adamization of Missing Link

10-2 is the scientific version of the event. Obviously the artist lacks the talent of a Michelangelo. Link assumes the same position as in Michelangelo's depiction, with arm and index finger extended having just been struck or about to be struck by a bolt from the impersonal God of Power and Light. Fortunately for us, link's mommy never warned him not to take cover under a tree during a thunderstorm, as a result, his brain has been or is about to be rewired. Although he has already acquired the cognitive functions, they are slow. The lightning did or will speed them up as he adapts to the beneficial short circuiting. In addition, that Bolt of Power added executive functions together with free will, conscience and creativity and along with that creativity, dreaming. He was endowed with a unique status among all other beasts. In the beginning link was hairy, pot-bellied and didn't smell very nice. (Biology doesn't always look nice or smell good.) He spoke a strange dialect devoid of all vowels, making it difficult to articulate even the shortest words and uncomplicated ideas. Link's situation was so bad that there was only room for improvement; it couldn't get worse, it could only get better, which it did by following the evolutionary law that was to be discovered 250,000 ± 50,000 years later by Charles Darwin and Alfred Russel Wallace.

What is it that separates man from beast? We still have a lot in common with our beastly hominid cousins: we are all hairy, we all are warm blooded, we are all born alive and are all nourished with milk. We differ in that we have free will, conscience and creativity. We have exchanged the survival of the physically fittest of Darwin for creativity, which in the waking or dream state is, without a doubt, more beneficial for survival – a good trade-off. The following trade-offs have been necessary to increase our chances of survival in our ascent from beast to man:

- Some brute strength was traded off for intelligence.
- Some of the no thinking of instinct and the fast thinking of intuition was traded off for the slow thinking of free will, conscience and creativity.
- Some of the unbridled instinctual behavior was traded off for the power of conscience.
- Some of that wonderfully refreshing dreamless sleep was traded off for dreaming.

Since dreaming has been so valuable an asset that has served us so reliably well up to this point in our evolutionary journey, nature has not yet selected anything better for which to trade it off. Although none of our brutish survival tools were traded-off completely, all of these trade-offs enhanced our survival.

The 1996 Nobelist, Wislava Shymborska, in her poem, *In Praise of Feeling Bad about Yourself,* suggests:

> *On this third planet of the Sun,*
> *among the signs of bestiality,*
> *a clear conscience is number one.*

Conscience, which implies free will, makes the difference. Beasts are predators; it is in their nature to mutilate and kill without guilt. Some humans with beastly behavior frequently claim a clear conscience. Those three attributes, (free will, conscience and creativity), that separate man from beast, most likely did not occur simultaneously but in a stepwise, evolutionary fashion.

We have to admit to what at this point *seems* obvious, that there is evolution, and it has been designed with the goal of Homo sapienship by using adaptation as a tool.

Once Homo sapienship has been reached, what next? Does evolution cease or do we continue to evolve into those sci-fi aliens with enormous cranial vaults, huge eyes and miniscule trunks and appendages? Having survived this far, how will we continue to assure our survival? There are predators out there of the same species or different species ready to strike at the most opportune moment when we are asleep and not even having the knowledge of our existence. The fourth miracle, our homosapienship with its creativity, is our protector. We have been passive recipients of the benefits of these miracles of life, evolution and creativity, but now the time has come when we must be active participants in the use of creativity in our quest for survival.

Creativity is universal for Homo sapiens. It is beneficial for Homo sapiens, it has unlimited applications, its primary utility is survival, its secondary is comfort and pleasure. Creativity is a gift. Homo sapiens did not create his own creativity, it was given to him.

In the beginning of the movie, *2001*, an ape (missing link) in the midst of a ferocious argument between two groups of apes who are shouting threats and curses in their vowelless language, mindlessly picks up a femur and suddenly, becoming aware of his creativity, uses it as a weapon to assure his survival and the survival of his progeny. It happened either by design or accident (whatever you want to believe) that the creativity of Homo sapiens became increasingly necessary for survival as life became more complicated. (More than nourishment became necessary since we were archea or eukarya 3.5 billion years ago.)

Mother Nature was solely charged with our survival until we achieved Homo sapienship with its creativity, at which point we were obliged to share that responsibility. With our ever changing environment, we used our creativity to adapt to our needs associated with survival. And we required more creativity to survive those products of creativity that have become harmful to us rather than beneficial. Creativity must always remain active, and it does. We use it numerous times during the day and at night to make those life-saving dreams. In dreamless sleep, where self-awareness is absent, there is no creativity.

Darwin, in spite of the fact that cognitive functions such as perceiving, thinking and remembering contribute a great deal to survival, focused most of his attention on the evolution of physical characteristics. It was Wallace who indicated more interest in the intellectual and moral. Although we would like to know at what point self-awareness arrived on the scene, at what point memory, at what point thinking, at what point creativity, at what point free will and conscience, at what point dreaming, it makes no difference if we don't. It is only of academic interest. Our knowledge or lack thereof does not change the progression of evolution.

Since dreams are universal, which means that only dreamers survived, then dreams must be necessary for survival. Those who had no dreams did not survive.

Whether in the jungles of Borneo or in the wilds of New York City, we are most vulnerable to predatory attack when we are asleep and, more specifically, when we are in dreamless sleep. When we are awake, say, sixteen of twenty-four hours, we have the advantage of the most important survival tool of awareness. When we are asleep and dreaming, we have that most important survival tool for about two hours, which leaves us with six hours in dreamless sleep when we are without it, unguarded, totally vulnerable.

Let's assume that 250,000 years ago the mortality rate of Homo sapiens living in the jungles of Africa by attacks of predators during eight hours of *dreamless* sleep would be 100%, then with ¼ of sleep time used in lighter *dream* sleep with its accompanying awareness, the mortality rate during sleep time would be decreased to 75% so that the survival rate would be 25%. That kind of decrease in mortality as the result of dream sleep over the millennia might well be just enough to assure survival of our species. The increase in survival, as described above, is exaggerated, but keep in mind that even a very small increase in survival over many generations could make the difference between extinction and survival of a species. As the result of the daytime awareness plus dream sleep awareness and in spite of the many natural and man-made catastrophes we are now here 7.2 billion strong.

We have succeeded in survival with plenty to spare, thanks to other devices that assure survival, such as clubs and spears, bows and arrows, dwellings, locks and keys, guns, clans, walled cities, police forces, armies and electronic security systems, all products of man's creativity. So, why do we still need to dream? We still need to dream because nocturnal predators remain a threat, although far less so with the increasing hi-tech security systems. We may reach the point where these systems are so reliable and efficient that dreaming will become unnecessary and fade away. We would enjoy eight hours of dreamless sleep, or perhaps, since dreamless sleep is more energizing than dream sleep, six hours of dreamless sleep would be sufficient to energize us enough to accomplish the tasks of every-day living effic-iently. Many of us would be happy to make such a trade-off for dreaming.

Dreams can be pleasant, neutral, unpleasant or night-marish. Nightmares are dress rehearsals for anticipated pred-atory attacks from humans, beasts or demons. In many, if not most, of our nightmares we wisely choose flight over fight as far as predators are concerned; that is our plan. When we are awake, we frequently have fears of predatory attacks that may occur while we are in that waking state and going about our business, and we make plans to deal with such attacks. Most of the time, our basic plan has to do with avoidance rather than confrontation. Since we frequently have such daytime thoughts, it is understandable that from time to time they may appear as nightmarish dream content with avoidance taking the form of desperate flight rather than fight. There is nothing better than such a dream dress rehearsal to prepare us for the real thing. Another tactic for dealing with predators in our nightmares is to bluff them into thinking that we are not frightened of them by making loud vocal threats, implying that we have a weapon and are prepared to use it unless they cease and retreat from their evil intent. Usually that tactic ends up with our bed mate waking us up when awakened by our screaming.

In the course of evolution, dreaming has become an important survival tool; it reliably guarantees self-awareness in sleep just as self-awareness in sleep guarantees dreaming.

While we are at it, let us not underestimate snoring as a protective phenomenon (almost like the loud vocal threat mentioned above) that Mother Nature has supplied most of us with during sleep to keep predators at a distance. What was one hundred and one pounds of fun at 9 P.M. has, at midnight, turned into a snorting, snarling, growling, three hundred pound tigress. She has become protective to the death of herself and her brood from all predators. She gets restful sleep while scaring off predators without even trying – an excellent survival tool. Being that our ears are located only a few centimeters away from our epiglottis and vocal cords, it is peculiar that we don't hear ourselves snore, and yet we can hear others snoring who are sleeping in another room with the door closed. What would happen if we were awakened by our own snoring? – Catastrophe.

PART THREE

HOW WE GET THERE

Chapter 11

REM SLEEP

"Dreaming permits each and every one of us to be
quietly and safely insane every night of our lives."
W. Dement

REM (rapid eye movement) sleep, which I prefer to think of as safety sleep, is identified by the following characteristics that are observable:

- Rapid movements of the eyeballs and twitching of the small muscles of the eyes, mouth, hands and feet,
- Paralysis of the large muscles of the extremities,
- Engorgement of erectile tissue,
- Specific EEG pattern and
- Shallower sleep.

and the following characteristics that are only experienced by the dreamer and are not observable:

- Awareness of one's existence
- Dreams.

The observable characteristics are frequently seen in man and other mammals, especially in pets and animals in sleep laboratories connected to devices such as EEGs, electro-myographs, plethysmographs and PET (positron emission tomography) scanners. When we observe these character-istics, we assume that they are intimately related to and indicate the mental experiences characteristic of awareness of existence and dreaming.

The relationship between REM sleep and remembered dreams is not clear cut. About 80% of remembered dreams are experienced during REM sleep while 20 % are exper-ienced in a non-REM stage of sleep. Certainly, one is more apt to be dreaming during REM sleep rather than any other of the sleep stages. REM sleep even in humans does not necessarily indicate the presence of a dream although it increases the probability. Admittedly, considering how rapidly dreams are forgotten, the dreaming during REM may be 100%. Another possibility is that the, so called, immediately forgotten dreams were thought dreams without visual mem-ories. (Chapter 12)

If this kind of uncertainty exists in humans, who are able to report remembered dreams or at least that they had experienced a dream, consider the degree of uncertainty in the case of non-speaking mammals that are unable to report dream content or even the act of dreaming. Observing small muscle contractions in Fido or Puss, at this point, can only be regarded as a curiosity – not necessarily a dream.

On an unseasonably warm day in early November 2009, in southern Fairfield County in Connecticut, there was a locust-like invasion of ladybugs, also known as Asian lady beetles. Homes were dotted with thousands of these attrac-tive insects. They are orange-red with black spots. Their beauty is a survival tool since birds have been taught by their moms, learned by experience or inherited the knowledge that colorful insects don't taste good. (Can you imagine a worm tasting better than a gorgeous ladybug?) Their attractiveness is further attested to by the fact that they are copied and manufactured into much enlarged versions as popular toys for toddlers and amusement park rides for kids of all ages.

They are very cooperative to observation under a stereo-microscope. Their undersides are as ugly as their topsides are pretty. The undersides look slimy and as scary as the monsters one frequently sees in sci-fi movies, their mouths grinding away, readying to devour anything in sight. However, they do not bite or sting; they don't seem to carry deadly bacteria. They are slow moving. They are willing to crawl harmlessly over one's fingers and hands. Periodically they uncover their hidden wings for short distance flights. They respond to light, sound and touch. They spend a great deal of time sleeping day or night, supine or prone and always with their lidless compound eyes fixed. They have no rapid eye movements because they have no extra ocular muscles. However, observing them at sleep and under the microscope, one can see periodic twitching of the pincers at the distal ends of their six appendages, homologous to the thumbs and index fingers of humans. It is difficult to believe that these cute/ugly creatures are having dreams just because they periodically exhibit small muscle contraction of their "fingers" during sleep. So, we must be careful in making the claim, in animals other than man, that any observable part of REM sleep is evidence of a dream in progress. We will never know until Fido tells us that he had a great dream last night of feasting on a dinosaur's femur.

In such biological situations where relationships are evident but too loose, we should consider the possibility of continuing evolution or devolution. For example, when an animal has feathers and wings we assume that it can fly, an extremely erroneous assumption when we consider ostriches, emus, kiwis and penguins, all of which have wings and feathers but cannot fly. They are flightless birds whose evolution into flyers has come to a halt; they will never succeed as flyers. It is possible but unlikely that they had been flyers at one time but lost that ability, and their wings and feathers have atrophied and became vestigial. Considering the survival of the fittest, a halt in evolution rather than devolution would have been more likely.

My claim is that although Fido exhibits observable characteristics of REM sleep, he is not necessarily dreaming. The characteristics that we observe may be preparations for the further evolution of Fido into a dreamer if his evolution were to continue. Although Fido is a fine animal, faithful, intelligent, with a good memory, aware of his existence and an REM sleeper, he lacks creativity, a powerful and necessary component for dreaming (remember $D = mc^n$.) and a distinguishing feature of Homo sapiens.

Also consider the observations of experimentalists who have recorded REM sleep in third trimester human fetuses in utero. What does a fetus remember? What is its capacity for creativity? Does REM in such a case indicate dreaming, or is it preparation for dreaming? *Could it be that the EEG tracing of REM sleep may not be so much a sign of dreaming as it is a sign of awareness of existence?* That could be a logical explanation for that twenty percent absence of dreams during REM sleep. As for the twenty percent of reported dreams during non-REM sleep, they may be the memories of dreams the subjects have had at one time during REM sleep which are involuntarily brought to mind by the request or suggestion of the researcher.

Being that observable evolutionary changes require tens or hundreds of thousands of years, we do not know if evolution has stopped with Homo sapiens as its ultimate goal or if Mother Nature is continuing to pursue super-humanhood. If, on the one hand, further progress toward survival has been entrusted to man through his gift of creativity then further evolution would no longer be considered necessary and would come to a halt. On the other hand, if man's creativity is insufficient in assuring survival and we require that evolution continues, we should be able to find many missing links living and well among us, not just in Africa and primate zoos but all over the planet. That hairy, muscular, apish looking guy at the beach, the one surrounded by all the pretty girls, may be one of them. Accordingly, we should be revisited in time and under certain conditions by currently extinct species. We should see again some real, honest to goodness dinosaurs, not just puny birds.

Rapid eye movements may be the mechanism for inducing the production of photons by chemical reactions in the vitreous body or the retina of the eyeball. These photons may be used to make the memories of which dreams are made to appear real. An in depth discussion of this hypothesis together with simple experiments will follow in the chapter on light.

Claims have been made that the rapid eye movements are an indication that the dreamer is following movement in the dream. The evidence for this seems to be slim. Rapid eye movements persist whether or not there is movement in the dream. Furthermore, why would a mental phenomenon, such as a dream call in the aid of the physical to verify the action of its hallucination?

Paralysis of the large muscles of the extremities is a protective mechanism that prevents the dreamer from injuring himself while fleeing from the dreamed of pursuing predator. The paralysis immediately disappears on waking so as not to interfere, if need be, with flight from an actual nearby predator.

Engorgement of erectile tissue during REM sleep in both sexes is puzzling. This relationship exists not only in dreams with sexual content but, apparently, with all or almost all dreams, even dreams of your severely arthritic grandmother tap dancing like Fred Astaire on a pew in St. Peter's Basilica. Many of us who have been lucky to have been born are the result of Dad, waking from a dream, still engorged and ready for procreation.

During REM sleep we exhibit a specific EEG pattern. The EEG pattern for REM sleep, which is the stage when dreaming is most likely to occur, has the closest resemblance to the EEG tracings that we see in the waking and light sleep stages (Figure 11). It supports what is obvious to anyone who has ever had a dream, that there is increased mental activity in dreaming resembling the mental activity of the waking state. It implies self-awareness, increased alertness, lighter sleep, greater safety and improved protection against a predatory attack. Temporary insanity is a worthwhile tradeoff for survival.

We frequently awaken from our last dream of the night in a state of reverie which is a pleasant mixture of snippets of dream and logical thinking. It is similar to daydreaming. We are aware that we are awake. However, our eyelids are heavy and feel as if they were glued together, but we like that feeling and do not make the effort to open them. Perhaps our eyes are enjoying the rest from the rapid eye movements during the dream. In addition, we experience what feels like a mild paresis of the limbs, not at all an unpleasant feeling, which may be the residual of the paralysis of the muscles of our extremities that occur in dreams; the chemicals that are responsible for that dream paralysis may not have been completely used up. This reverie lasts for five or ten minutes, and because it is pleasant, we have the urge to prolong it. However, laziness guilt and the need to be on time for work breaks the spell, and we reluctantly leave that pleasant state. Our "lazy bones", after some stretching, become invigorated and ready to cope with surviving the day.

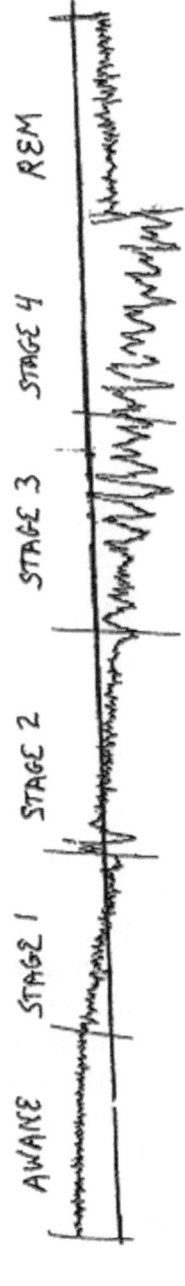

Figure 11 A collage of EEG tracings of typical sleep stages. The straight line indicates the division between wakefulness and sleep. It illustrates the progression from awake through the stages of light sleep and deep sleep to REM sleep. Notice the similarity between REM sleep and awake and light sleep stages 1 and 2. The transition between awake and light sleep is gradual as is the transition between light and deep sleep stages 3 and 4 but abrupt between deep and REM sleep. The EEG tracing in REM sleep may be considered an indication of the dreamer's feelings of self-awareness.

Chapter 12

LIGHT

"Nature and nature's laws laid hid in night.
God said, 'Let Newton be!' and all was light."
                                        A. Pope

One sleepless night in 2010 Lady Serendipity visited me with photons just as she had visited Freud with symbols in 1895, Aserinsky with REM sleep in 1951 and LaBerge with a lucid dream in 1967.

While tossing and turning in bed, I felt the pillow gently pressing against my eye. At the same time, I noticed a brief, circular flash of light. I tried and was successful in reproducing it, at first with the pillow and then with my finger. Although I had been an insomniac for decades, it was the first time that I became aware of such an event which, surely, had come and gone unnoticed by me for thousands of times. Since then, experiment has led to experiment and more experiments until a new theory of dreaming emerged – *The Twin Photon Theory*.

Proud grandparents are often heard to exclaim, "He (she) is so smart it's scary." Such hyperbole frequently occurs when viewing the Crayola drawings of their three, four or five year old, mainly firstborn, grandchildren. The talent in question is one of manipulating photons into two dimen-sional colored images of three-fingered Mommy and Daddy, a house, Daddy's car, and purple, five-legged Fido with green dinosaur's teeth – exceptional feats.

More exceptional and without effort on the part of the dream artist of any age, is the ability to manipulate existing internal photons into images that we can't tell from the real McCoy. Amazingly, they are not two dimensional but 3D, and even more amazing, because of the relationship of motion to time, they are 4D (three spatial and one time dimension), which creates the illusion of reality. Individuals suffering from psychosis or delirium (DTs and others) are able to manipulate photons in the waking state into images such as snakes, insects, all kinds of predators, angels, God, etc., all of which have that 4D quality of reality which, at times, may lead to bizarre behavior or even death in an attempt to flee imagined malevolent predators.

All light comes from the Sun and stars either directly or indirectly. When we look at the Sun and stars, the light enters our eyes directly without any intermediary except for the atmosphere. Otherwise, most of the seeing we do is of reflected light, photons from the Sun and stars that bounce off material objects and into our eyes. The light from fire, light bulbs, flashlights, candles, sparks, television, certain mushrooms and lightning bugs also enters our eyes directly but can be reflected as well, just as the light from the Sun and stars. Like the Sun and stars, these devices have stores of photons which are released under certain conditions. Come to think of it, all matter has stored photons, the moon, the planets, molecules, atoms, you and me – everything. Most objects have not reached those certain conditions whereby the stored photons are released in quantities sufficient to be detected by the human eye, e.g., wood must be burned to release its stored photons and heat. The brightness of light experienced is directly proportional to the number of photons and their wavelengths entering our eye through the pupil.

Our eyes have been gifted with the ability to sense light but at the limited wavelengths of the visual spectrum.

Our senses, in view of their capacity to receive specialized signals from without, inform the brain of conditions in the outside world, information that is necessary for survival. Our eyes are the instruments that allow external photons to enter and stimulate the specialized cells of the retina that allow us to perceive the forms, movements and colors of external objects. Simple experiments show us that all photons do not arrive directly from the outside world, but some have been stored in the eyeball and can be released by its deformation. Photons are photons no matter where they come from. They are transformed into the electrical signals that go to the visual cortex in the back of the brain where *all* seeing is done. The photons that enter directly from the outside are already formed into recognizable images, while the photons that come out of storage are nebulous raw material, ready to be molded into the images that we experience in dreams.

Two interesting sources of direct rather than reflected light are the Jack O'Lantern mushroom, very common and very poisonous, and the lightning bug (firefly). Apparently, the Jack O'Lantern emits photons at night most likely to attract certain insects for pollination, while the lightning bug periodically emits photons, not to prevent it from bumping into objects in the dark, but to attract a gorgeous mate. Their photons have been stored in a biochemical and released periodically. The time interval between the flashes of the lightning bug and the glow of the mushroom is most likely determined by the rate at which the chemicals have been used up and then restored; for the lightning bug it would be every few seconds, for the mushroom it may be every twenty four hours.

Photons, which are the massless quantum particles that carry light, can be supplied by biochemical reactions within the eye. This can be easily demonstrated by the pressure/lateral gaze experiment illustrated in Figure 12-1 b, c.

We literally have at our fingertips access to an optical lab where, with uncomplicated experiments, we can release photons stored within us. (Of interest, these experiments also demonstrate the presence of the optic chiasm, the crossing of some fibers of the optic nerves to the opposite side without cracking open the skull and examining the underside of the brain.)

After we have been in a dark room for a few minutes, with eyes closed and gazing laterally (either to the right or left), if we exert gentle finger pressure on the *medial* aspect of the eyeball of the eye gazing away from the nose, we will see in the same eye, in the direction of push, concentric circles of light or poorly formed light flashes. (Figure 12-1 b Medial Pressure/Lateral Gaze Experiment.) This is an indication that the mechanical pressure we exert results in a chemical reaction within the cells of the retina that cause them to produce light (photons). If we repeatedly apply pressure, the chemicals involved in the reaction will be depleted, and the light will disappear only to reappear when the chemicals have been restored with time, less than a minute. The light we visualize in the concentrics is scintillating not fixed. Most likely the scintillations are due to the frequency of the absolute and relatively refractory periods of the neurons carrying the photons, now transformed into electrical impulses, to the back of the brain.

The scientific name for the scintillating circles is "phosphenes". I prefer to use the more descriptive "scintillating concentric circles" throughout this chapter.

For a brighter vision of the scintillating concentric circles, after a few minutes of rest, with eyes closed again, and gazing to the left, put gentle pressure on the *lateral* aspect of the right eye, if gazing to the right, put gentle pressure on the *lateral* aspect of the left eye. (Figure 12-1c Lateral Pressure/Lateral Gaze Experiment.) Amazingly, you will see clear and beautiful, multi-colored, scintillating, concentric circles, again in the direction of push but not in the eye you are pressing but in the opposite eye.

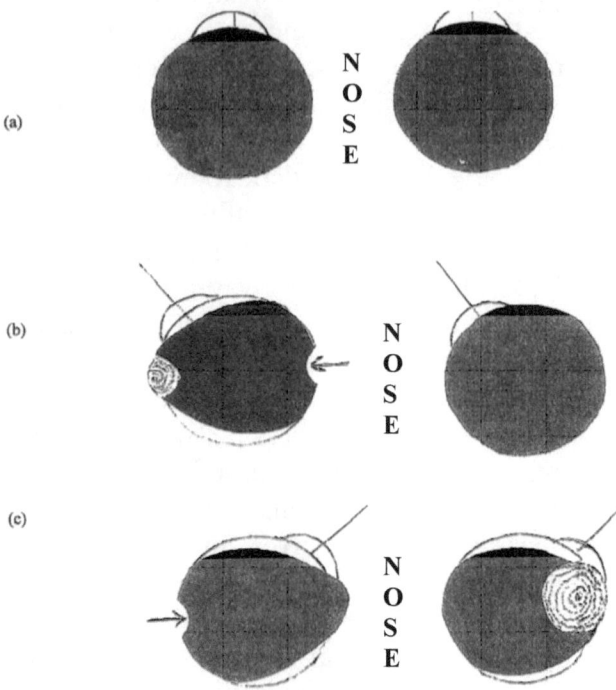

Figure 12-1 This is an exaggerated illustration of how the eyeball is deformed by finger pressure *and* the tug of extra-ocular muscles, producing scintillating concentric circles (phosphenes) in the visual field. (a) Two dimensional representations of eyeballs at rest and gazing forward. (b) Medial finger pressure with lateral gaze to left indicates where the direction of push will cause scintillations to appear in the *same* eye. (c) Lateral finger pressure with gaze to right indicates where the direction of push will cause scintillations to appear in the *opposite* eye because of the splitting of the optic nerve at the optic chiasm.

Seeing the circles in the eye opposite to the one pressured is explained by the splitting and course of the optic nerves at the optic chiasm. (Figure 12-2.) The visual cortex on the side opposite to the eye that is being deformed sees the image as originating from the *undeformed* retina and vitreous, and because of the lack of deformation there, the concentrics are more symmetrical and brilliant.

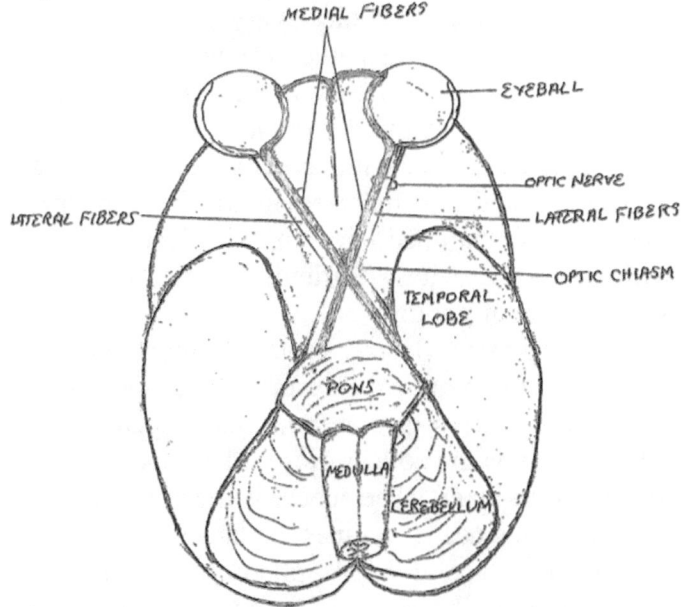

Figure 12-2 This is a diagram of the underside of the brain. The medial fibers of the optic nerves cross at the optic chiasm and eventually arrive at the visual cortex in the occipital lobes of the opposite sides. The lateral fibers do not cross and eventually arrive at the visual cortex of the occipital lobes on the same sides. Without this arrangement we would have two separate visual fields without the fusion into one that we have become accustomed to. The cross over explains how deforming one eyeball results in an image of concentric circles in the other. The visual area in the occipital lobe cannot be shown in the figure because it lies on top of the cerebellum.

Why are photons stored and released in this fashion? What is the use? The light produced in this experiment is direct not reflected, and it is produced by the deformation of the eyeball causing the release of photons from the rods and cones of the retina where they are stored in a biochemical molecule. The determining factor appears to be the deformation of the eyeball. But note that the finger pressure alone is not enough to produce that nice, very bright image of the scintillating circles that we perceive when we combine the pressure with lateral gaze. To see those dazzling scintillating concentrics one requires the deformation of the eyeball provided by pressure together with lateral gaze; a greater amount of deformation with its increase in mechanical energy is necessary. As we shall see later on, with just a lateral gaze and without pressure it is difficult but not impossible to detect the release of photons.

While the pressure/lateral gaze is maintained, the scintillating concentrics will last four or five seconds. When the pressure/lateral gaze is discontinued and repeated again in about three seconds the concentrics will reappear.

According to Plato, "The sphere is the most perfect of all geometric shapes, since it confines the largest possible volume within a given surface area." A sphere, like the shape of an eyeball, is the most efficient form for enclosing a given space, and when it is deformed in any way, either by pressure or by being tugged upon, its contents will be forced to occupy a smaller space, thereby increasing the concentration of its contents (gas, liquids, photons or other particles). Since the production of light in these experiments is proportional to the deformation of the eyeball, then the greater the deformation the brighter the light. When we do the pressure/lateral gaze maneuver, the total deformation is that caused by pressure plus the tug on the eyeballs by the medial and lateral rectus muscles. (The other external ocular muscles are the superior and inferior recti for up and down movement of the eyeball and the superior and inferior obliques which allow us to fix our eyes on a target object when we move our head, without any effort – amazing.)

When we bump our head while trying to fix the leak under the kitchen sink, we see "stars" (sudden bursts of light). It is the rapid release of photons due to the sudden, momentary deformation of the eyeballs. (Borrowing the quantum language of Neils Bohr, we might say that any deformation of the eyeball, whether by push or pull, if rapid enough, will pressure the electrons into a lower orbital shell with the release of photons – his literal quantum jump.) Eye movements must be rapid in order to produce a sufficient number of photons necessary for a visual image. Making *gradual* contact with a boxer's fist or a pipe under the sink will never make us see "stars". If one performs the pressure/lateral gaze experiment with gradual pressure there will be no scintillating concentrics. The speed and extent of deformation appear to be the determining factors in the release of photons which allow us to perceive light.

Isaac Newton (1642-1727) was obsessed with light and performed light experiments but, as far as is known, he was not especially interested in dreams. He was determined to unlock nature's best kept secrets involving light, gravity and mathematics He is best remembered for his inverse square (also claimed by Hooke) and the calculus (also claimed by Leibnitz). Shortly after he received his bachelor's degree from Trinity College at Cambridge, his first scientific achievement was the decomposition and recomposition of white light with the aid of prisms.

It is difficult to imagine that a man of such brilliance would deliberately incise the extreme corner of his eye in the performance of some kind of optics experiment, a dumb thing to do even for individuals with single digit I.Q.s. We know he was a religious man, actually a theologian (but not a nice one). Perhaps his eye had offended him, and he was trying to pluck it out with the aid of a sharp instrument, having interpreted the Bible too literally. We also wonder if this man with a history of psychosis, perhaps due to schizophrenia or mercury poisoning from his alchemy, was responding to a command auditory hallucination to perform that kind of self-mutilation. Evidently, what he did had no effect on his vision, nor did it cause strabismus or any other observable disfigurement; what he did, he must have done carefully.

There is no documentation of this gruesome experiment. If it was carried out to completion, one would guess it was unsuccessful, otherwise, it would have gained the same degree of notoriety as being hit on the head with a falling apple. We don't know when he performed this experiment, but, probably, it preceded the publication of his *Optics* in 1730.

Apparently, he guided the lancet along the bony structure of the orbit, thereby avoiding damage to the soft tissue of the eye. One suspects his goal was to deform the eyeball from behind. Being a keen observer, most likely he was well aware of the pressure/lateral gaze experiment and the importance of the direction of push in determining the position of the scintillating concentric images, as described above. The pain must have been excruciating, unless he used some sort of local anesthetic, cocaine for example. (It wasn't purified until the 1880s when it began to be used in ophthalmic surgery, but its anesthetic properties were known to Peruvian Indians probably centuries before, when it was used as a local anesthetic in trephining procedures.)

Almost certainly, Newton's folly started out as a bona fide experiment and not the result of an all too literal interpretation of the Bible or of a command auditory hallucination. As a scientist, in all probability, he was not completely satisfied with his observations of direction of push and was looking for more stringent verification. Most likely he reasoned that if pressure was applied to the back of the eyeball, light would be released outwardly through the pupil (as frequently seen in some villains in horror movies, for example, the Morlocks in *The Time Machine*). He might even be able to see scintillating concentrics. This could easily be viewed in a darkened room with the aid of a mirror. (Ancient Greeks believed that the mechanism of vision consisted of a beam of light being projected through the pupil of the eye illuminating the target object.) Most likely, he made a small incision at the lateral corner of the eye but went no further with the lancet. If, in spite of the pain, he was able to further carry on with the experiment, he may have introduced a curved, blunt probe, inserted it to the point where it reached the back of the eye, at least that was his intention, and manipulated it to produce varying degrees of pressure outwardly and through the lens. (Figure 12-3)

DON'T TRY THIS EXPERIMENT AT HOME
OR ANYWHERE ELSE.

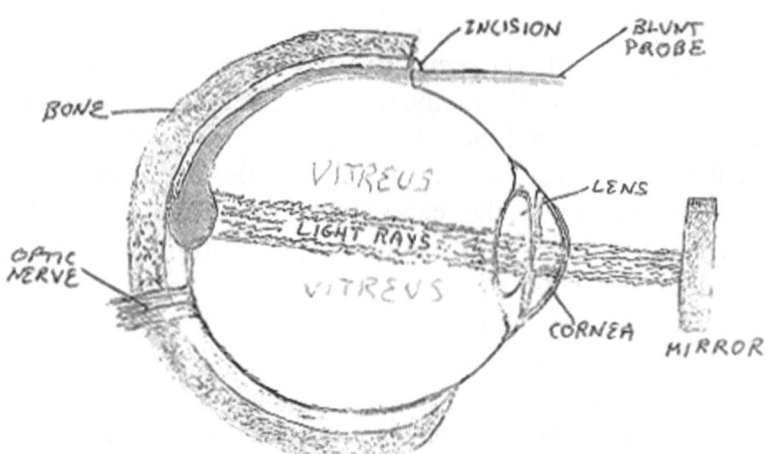

Figure 12-3 Newton's Eye. Horizontal section through the left eyeball and the optic nerve. Newton probably inserted a blunt probe through an incision he made with a lancet at the lateral corner of his left eye. He threaded the probe between the bony structure of the orbit and the eyeball to the back of the eye in an attempt to exert pressure from behind releasing light through the pupil to be viewed in a mirror.

Since the luminescence of lightning bugs persists for a while after they have been squashed dead (You did that when you were a kid, didn't you?), a better approach would have been for Newton to carefully remove the eyeball of a freshly slaughtered pig and pushed from back to front to observe the presence of light production.

Examining the scintillating circles more closely, we see that there are about five concentrics, and they spin clockwise in the left eye and counterclockwise in the right eye. They may consist of a single color or a combination of any of the colors of the visual spectrum. The diameter of the outside circles, I would estimate to be about 1.5 centimeters (about the size of a nickel). As soon as pressure or lateral gaze is released, they immediately disappear. If both are sustained, the concentrics will persist for about three or four seconds. If this maneuver (pressure) is rapidly repeated over and over again the concentrics will appear for diminishing periods of time until, finally, the chemical becomes depleted and nonreactive, and the circles fail to appear no matter how great the pressure. After a rest period, the entire maneuver can be repeated with the reappearance of the concentrics. The time required for the restoration of full reactivity is less than five seconds. This off and on scheduling is reminiscent of the lightning bug signaling. With the lightning bug it occurs automatically since it is a pre-programmed biological machine.

One wonders if the photon production that we have been discussing also occurs automatically during REM sleep since, during REM, one of the components for the production of photons is present, namely the rapid deformation of the eyeball by the to and fro tugging of the extra ocular muscles. It is possible that the deformation alone (without external pressure), caused by the extra-ocular muscles alternately pulling on the eyeball, might be enough to release photons if the movements were rapid enough and prolonged enough. Consequently, with my eyes closed, I tried to mimic the rapid eye movements of dream sleep to see if I was able to produce some light in my visual fields.

After several failures, I discovered that, indeed, rapid eye movements alone were able to release photons but in very limited quantities, hardly noticeable, not in the amounts necessary to form the bright scintillating concentrics. The photon releases were unpredictable – *but they were there.*

After dark adaptation is complete by being in a very dark room for about thirty minutes, then with eyes closed, if one moves the eyes rapidly back and forth one may notice very faint images similar to crescent moons with their horns pointing in the direction of the rapid eye movement. They can be seen very briefly for only one to four passes after which they disappear. The brightness of the crescents fades with each pass. (A pass is when the eyeballs move past the midline of gaze.) On one occasion I was successful in producing crescent moons for six passes and on another for ten passes. Rapid eye movements alone are able to release photons but in barely visible amounts. For good reason the crescent moons associated with rapid eye movements are not very bright. Imagine how distracting and annoying it would be if they were bright enough to visualize during the daytime as we rapidly move our eyes from one object to another.

If one, with or without having successfully visualized the crescent moons, does rapid eye movements for about ten seconds then performs the pressure/lateral gaze maneuver, one will notice the absence or marked dimming of the scintillating concentrics, which is an indication that rapid eye movements, in spite of their slight (weak) deformation of the eyeballs, are able to "steal" photons from the concentrics.

Those barely visible crescent moons are important because they suggest that rapid eye movements, produced voluntarily in the dark, when we are awake, are able to squeeze sufficient photons out of the electrochemical molecules of the retinal cells when we are asleep, and they may be used in the construction of the visual images of dreams.

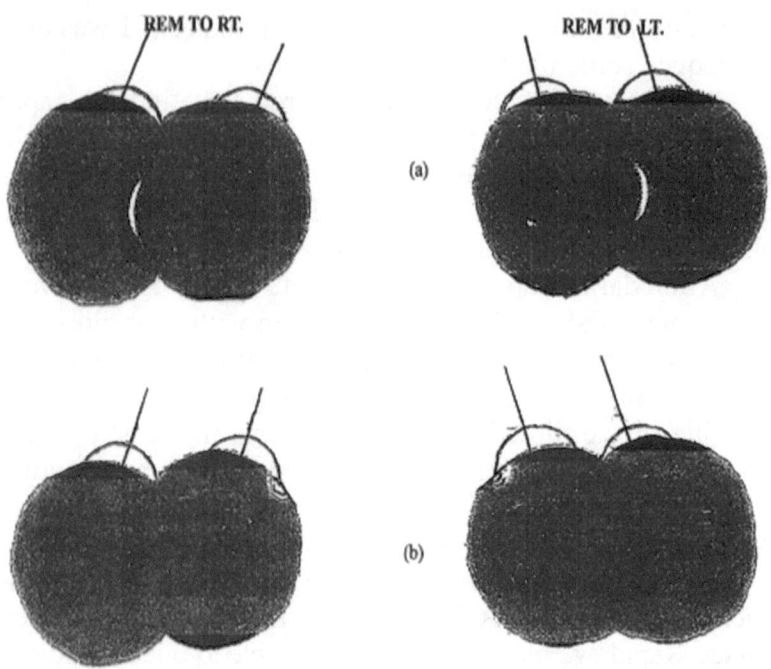

Figure 12-4 Visual Fields (a) Shows the position of the crescent moon images while awake and with eyes *lightly* closed when voluntary rapid eye movements are to the right and to the left. The images are difficult to visualize because they are brief in duration and seldom occur after the first one to four passes. (b) The position of partial scintillating circles as they appear with voluntary rapid eye movements with eyes *tightly* closed.

We wonder how a few crescent moons produced by REMs are able to provide enough light for a visual dream. It is by starting a chain reaction. The photons in a single spark from a campfire falling on dry vegetation can easily release huge amounts of photons stored in trees and brush during huge wildfires that light up the sky for miles. In a similar manner, a few photons from crescent moons liberate the many photons stored in the memory banks of the temporal lobes, lighting up the memories that we experience in dreams. In both instances a small amount of added energy starts the chain reaction.

If one performs the pressure/lateral gaze maneuver immediately after spontaneously awakening from a completed dream, one will notice that the scintillating concentrics have diminished significantly in brightness and are dark blue which may indicate that the photons have been almost all used up during the dream and have not had time enough to be replenished in the retina. The dark blue color, may indicate that the less energetic photons of the visual spectrum have been used up first during a dream.

If we deplete the electrochemical's ability to produce photons by repeating the pressure/lateral gaze maneuver over and over again in the same eye until the concentrics disappear and then repeat the pressure/lateral gaze with the other eye, the concentics will reappear in their usual brightness. This means that both eyes function independently in furnishing photons for the construction of concentrics. Consequently, an individual with unilateral blindness, depending on the pathology, will be able to produce concentrics.

An individual with acquired blindness, e.g., retinitis pigmentosa, is unable to see, but he can call upon his visual memories to construct a dream. They serve him as well as the sighted individual and decay at the same average rate. Since the visual memory in the individual with acquired blindness is unimpaired, he can bring to his mind's eye in the waking state the visual memories that he stored when he was sighted, and, when he is asleep, he has the same ability to dream as the sighted individual with the same feeling of reality. Photons have been stored with his visual memories and are available when they are necessary for visual dreams.

Individuals, blind since birth, will have no visual memories and, consequently, no visual dreams even though they may experience flashes of light. Their dream experiences are like their life experiences, the objects in their dreams are recognized by touch and sound memories and, perhaps, by smell and taste memories but not by visual memories.

The crescent moon experiment was rather disappointing for the sparse amount of light generated by voluntary rapid eye movements. Figure 12-4 b shows the light production when rapid eye movements are performed with eyes *tightly* closed. It is the increased pressure on the eyeball by the peripheral part of the orbicularis oculi muscle, which closes the eye forcibly. (The central part of the muscle closes the eye gently.)

Again, in this experiment, as in the others, eyeball pressure with its deformation is the significant factor in producing light. Occasionally, when yawning, which requires contraction of the orbicularis oculi muscles and the resulting deformation of the eyeballs, one may visualize light flashes.

The pressure in the eyeball can be increased from without, as we have been demonstrating up to now, or from within, say, as in the pathological condition of glaucoma. If there is an increase in the contents of the eyeball by too much stuff flowing in or not enough stuff flowing out or by dilatation of the blood vessels of the retina, there would be a pressure increase from within. Although in glaucoma there is increased pressure from within, it occurs gradually so that a significant number of photons are not produced suddenly, and light is not experienced as it is with sudden external pressure.

The extra-ocular muscles are voluntary muscles. They are under the control of the will when we are awake. However the contraction and relaxation of these muscles during REM sleep is involuntary – there is no action of the will. It is unusual (except in pathological conditions such as Parkinson's disease) that voluntary muscles move involuntarily for lengthy periods of time, not just an occasional muscle twitch.

Rapid eye movements during sleep are forced upon us by nature and so they must serve some important function.

Again we call upon the Copernican dictum that we depend upon to encourage and inspire us throughout this attempt to explain why and how light intrudes on the darkness of sleep.

".... We should rather follow the wisdom of nature,
which as it takes very great care not to have produced
anything superfluous or useless... "

We wonder what the purpose of periodic rapid eye movements is during sleep. We know that that the phenomenon is about 80% connected with dreaming, maybe even 100%. Do the REMs cause dreaming or does dreaming cause the REMs? While not the cause of the dream, do they provide something required for dreaming? Do they represent the voluntary eyeball movements of the dreamer following the action of the dream? Do they produce photons which may be necessary for dream imaging? Do they produce any photons at all? I think so.

What we see with eyeball deformation caused by rapid eye movements alone depends upon:

1. the number of photons transformed into electrical signals that reach the visual cortex in the occipital lobe which, in turn, depends upon the synchronization of the photon speeding at 300,000 kilometers/sec. with the electrical transmission speed of the neuron, 100 meters/sec.,
2. the absolute and relative refractory periods of the neuron,
3. the amount and concentration of the electrochemicals stored in the retina and
4. the phenomenon of averted vision which enables us to visualize dimly lit objects indirectly from the corner of the eye that we cannot see when viewed directly; a barely visible star becomes brighter if you don't look at it directly.

If the amount of photons released with rapid eye movements alone was the same as with the pressure/lateral gaze
maneuver, the appearance of crescent moons would be as
predictable and bright as the scintillating concentric circles.

When we do visualize the crescent moons, they will
occur when we first start the rapid eye movement exercise
with the first one to four passes. We start with the photons
synchronized enough with the electrical impulses, but rapidly
the synchronization disappears, and our occipital lobes no
longer see an image. It is not unusual for things to start in
sync and lose their synchronization after a while. Clocks do
it all the time.

It is interesting but not surprising that the light produced by voluntary rapid eye movements takes the form of
crescent moons since crescent moons are arcs of the
previously described scintillating circles. The shape of the
light images is unimportant since the photons, when they
interact with our dream memories, are reorganized to produce
the images we experience in dreams. The photons are the
raw material that is poured into the "molds" of our memories. (When things get mysterious, turn to quantum physics
for understanding or more mystery.)

Thought dreams are dreams that occur without benefit
of the visual images that photons produce. In thought
dreams we have all the properties of a visual dream but no
images. These dreams are more likely to occur during REM
sleep when the dreamer is aware of his existence. When the
dreamer awakens from such a dream, he knows that he has
been dreaming but has no memory of its content because no
images were visualized.

When we practice rapid eye movements while we are
awake and with eyes closed in an effort to mimic what
nature does in REM sleep, the natural automatic synchronization we experience in dreams is lost. Consequently,
the failure rate at visualizing the crescent moons is very
high; their appearance is erratic. However, that takes nothing

away from the observed relationship between eyeball deformation by rapid eye movements and photon production –
crescent moons are *never* seen when there are no rapid eye
movements.

Photons are transformed by specialized cells in the retina
into electrical signals that find their way to the occipital
lobes (a fair distance to travel) where they are perceived as
images. (Peculiarly, these images are experienced as if they
were in our eyes.) One wonders if the thought dreamer has
run out of photons or, more likely, did the electrical
impulses get short-circuited to the frontal lobes, where most
thinking is done, while they were on their way to the visual
cortex in the occipital lobes, where all seeing is done,
including the seeing that we experience in dreams. (*...the
wisdom of nature...often prefers to endow one thing with
many effects.*) If that is so then we would expect a lesion of
the occipital lobes not only to cause blindness but also to
prevent visual dreams. Hobson, from his personal experience
with stroke and dreamlessness, concludes that an intact
forebrain, which includes the occipital lobes, is necessary
for dreaming. Perhaps we can encourage neurosurgeons and
experimental neurophysiologists to confirm or deny that
theory.

Thought dreams are similar to daydreams since in neither
do we experience visual imagery. It may be that these are the
dreams in which we solve problems without any effort on
our part which would confirm theories that claim problem
solving as a utility of dreaming. If it is so, it may be the
primary utility of dreams or, at least, a very important secondary. Since amnesia is a property of thought dreams, we will
never know. Visual dreams are difficult to remember; thought
dreams are impossible. If we were to write an equation for
thought dreams, it would be $tD = c^n$. The c is simply the
creativity that is interwoven in all dreams but, in this case,
without visual memories, only a memory of existence.

Attempting to answer the important questions about the relationship between photons and REM sleep, I performed the following simple experiments: Because of my few experiences of being aware that I was dreaming while in the midst of a dream, perhaps because of a micro-awakening, I felt it was possible, if I awakened immediately at the end of a dream and kept my eyes closed, I might be able to continue the dream (similar to lucid dreaming). This did not occur, but I observed light in my visual field. My initial attempt resulted in the dream being immediately forgotten, and the light took the form of vague blue and white images which resembled scrambled eggs although scrambled eggs are yellow and white. Having repeated this experiment a number of times on different occasions with similar results except for the visualization of a *variety* of images including: lines and rows of yellow half-moons, measuring about three millimeters in diameter with sharp borders on a black background, a pile of white birch fire logs on a medium blue background, measuring about eighteen inches long with a diameter of about three inches with fairly sharp borders to begin with which quickly went out of focus, Arabic writing in white on a medium blue background, a Pollock-like collection of many colors, black crosses on a dark gray background lined up as one would see in a cemetery and a color map of the United States. These images, all with eyes closed and in color, appeared immediately after remembered or forgotten dreams, and lasted for about five seconds. Those images that followed *remembered* dreams had nothing to do with the dream content.

To make sure I was fully awake when I visualized these images and that they were not part of a dream, I gave myself the simple task of transferring my ring from the ring finger of my left hand to the little finger of my right hand as soon as I became aware of the images. That task, having been performed successfully, reinforced my perception that these images were experienced in the state of full wakefulness with my eyes closed; they were *hypnopompic* hallucinations. (Hypnogogic hallucinations are those occurring when one is *falling* asleep.) The content of hypnogogic hallucinations is variable but frequently with geometric forms. I was unable to find any connection between image content and dream content or image content and memories. They could not be reproduced by an act of the will; they occurred spontaneously and were self-organized. It is likely that most of us experience hypnopompic hallucinations but do not pay attention to them.

My next task was to determine if the images appeared immediately after I awakened from *non-dream* sleep with my eyes closed. They did not. And they did not even appear when I attempted to mimic the rapid eye movements of dreaming or even when I consciously tried to imagine them. It may be that in thought dreams we have run out of photons and so there are no visual images while in hypnopompic hallucinations there is an excess of unused photons from dreaming that spill over into the waking state.

At this point we cautiously conclude that:

- Any deformation of the eyeball, if rapid enough, will cause the release of stored photons proportional to the degree and speed of deformity.
- The light experienced in our dreams is not imaginary – it is a quantum phenomenon.
- Photons interact with visual memories to produce the visual images of dreams.
- REMs in dreams may produce photons that persist into the waking state with eyes closed.

The unique interaction of matter (the massless photon) with that which is non-matter (mind, memory, perception) is facilitated in dreams. They are close cousins who enjoy their regularly occurring nightly get togethers.

In response to a previously asked question, dreaming does not cause rapid eye movements. Our experiments indicate that it is more likely that rapid eye movements cause dreaming or, at least, rapid eye movements provide something necessary for dreaming; that would be photons necessary in the imaging of the visual memories in dreams.

Many of us are curious about the presence or absence of color in dreams. Because color or the lack thereof is a part of dream content as much as faces, places and things, it is just as unimportant. Color in dreams is determined by the same thing that determines color when we are awake – the number of photons and their wave lengths. In the waking state, we are, for the most part, continuously exposed to the full visual spectrum of light to the point of taking color for granted. We are unimpressed by color in the waking or dream states; we really don't pay much attention to the colors that surrounds us unless they are extraordinarily vivid as in certain sunsets, Technicolor movies, color television, fireworks, light shows, flowers, Hawaiian shirts and may-flower yellow Bugattis to name a few. If our dream content includes something vividly colorful, we designate it as a "color dream", otherwise, we are unimpressed, just as we are unimpressed by "ordinary" color in the waking state.

Colors in dreams are diluted by white light to such an extent that we rarely recognize them as color dreams. However, the few artists I have questioned (and as one would expect), because of their increased sensitivity to color, report much more color dreams than the non-artistic individual.

What seems to be a "black and white" dream, if one recalls it in detail, one will frequently find a hint of color, e.g., a red car in a parking lot filled with hundreds of cars of unimpressive color, yellow headlights of an approaching car where all else is black, the blue trim on a white dinner plate.

It is likely that *all* dreamers have color dreams *all* the time. White light is composed of red, blue and green light, the only colors that the cone cells in the retina were built to perceive. They are mixed, added and subtracted in such a way that they produce a huge variety of colors – the eye can see over 16 million colors. (No wonder Darwin "shuddered" when it came to the evolution of the eye.) Red, green and blue light may be diluted by the white light of their own making, to such an extent, that the occipital lobes are no longer able to distinguish the colors and experience them as the white of "black and white" dreams. The black of those dreams simply being the lack of the white. Consequently, most dreams are reported as black and white. So, although our eyes can see those millions of colors, our occipital lobes in dreams frequently cannot distinguish one from the other or color from black and white.

(N.B. Never confuse light color with paint color. Red, green and blue light, when combined produce white light; red, green and blue paint, when mixed, produce a murky grayish brown. Light colors behave altogether differently from paint colors.)

Technicolor movies are pretty and romantic but, obviously, a false representation of the world that surrounds us, and we readily recognize their unreality. In fact, although I enjoy Technicolor, it has been my experience that "black and white" movies give me more of a feeling of reality than does Technicolor. The absence or paucity of those vivid primary colors in dreams probably contributes much more to those feelings of reality that we experience in all of our dreams.

Many dream researchers, experimentalists and enthusiasts pay much attention to the significance of emotions in dreams. Anxiety is probably the most common emotion experienced in dreams, being that the most common themes in dreams are being lost, unprepared or chased. Emotions make dreams more interesting and more compelling to be watched, just as emotions in movies, plays and novels rivet the viewer's attention. Imagine the boredom in watching emotionless movies or plays or reading emotionless novels.

In addition, experiencing anxiety in dreams may ready us for the flight or fight response when we awaken and become aware of an approaching predator. As far as other emotions are concerned, they seem to have no more utility than dream content in general.

The work of Stephen LaBerge on lucid dreaming is of great interest to dream scientists and enthusiasts. He claims that, with a small amount of (expensive) lucid dream training, one can have a nightly vacation at the resort of his or her choice, win the lotto, wine and dine with celebrities of all sorts and engage in intimate relationships (not symbolically like Tom in Chapter 1). His training is directed at teaching the dreamer to recognize that he is in a dream and then manipulating the dream content into his desires. It is not unusual for successful lucid dreamers to enjoy hundreds of lucid dreams of their choosing. In ordinary dreams there is the automatic manipulation of photons to produce visual memories without any act of the will and totally uncontrolled. Lucid dreaming maintains that dream content can be manipulated and controlled by the will, without waking up, once we know that we are in a dream – certainly, a desirable skill.

Having had the experience once or twice a year of realizing that I was dreaming while in a dream, I noticed that the content of such dreams have always placed me in some nightmarish situation, and, as one would expect, having discovered it was only a dream, an immense sense of relief occurred to the point of euphoria. Many lucid dreamers describe euphoria as the result of their lucid dreams.

If the claims that lucid dreamers make that we can control our dreams are valid, it is easy to make a case for lucid dreaming to be included in the curricula of public school systems starting in kindergarten. Consider the many benefits that could result: the thirst for psychedelia would be quenched without the use of dangerous drugs, carnal desires would be satisfied without the fear of sexually transmitted diseases, those who feel inferior could enjoy celebrity, athletic prowess would be available for those physically challenged, aggressive impulses could be acted out without injury to anyone and many other good things desired by the dreamer. I would enjoy a taste of those utopian nights. Come to think of it, lucid dreaming seems to have a lot in common with *One Mind Theory* discussed in Chapter 4, where all that exists, is the product of one mind, yours. You are the creator of the universe as you want it to be.

One wonders why, when we are in the waking state, having more control of more accurate memories than in our dreams, more creativity than when dreaming with full power of the will to focus and with access to loads of photons, we are unable to reproduce in our memories the feelings of reality, of being there, as we experience them in dreams. I believe there are two simultaneously acting explanations: first, we are distracted by the inflow of perceptions through the five senses when we are awake and second, and more importantly, is the automatic correction that our logical mind imposes on that which defies logic. We enter the dream state from the deep sleep state with a clean slate. There is no distraction and no logical mind to prevent the construction of dreams with the tools of memory and creativity – NO MATTER HOW OUTRAGEOUS.

Chapter 13

THE TWIN PHOTON THEORY OF DREAMING

Herein lays the answer to all of your dreams.
JPR

Cosmologists have determined that the average mass density of the universe is one atom per cubic meter, while the average number of photons is 400 million per cubic meter. These are averages, and the actual amount of atoms and photons depends on the location in space where the counting is being done. These numbers would be higher in galaxies and zero or close to it in the vast areas of intergalactic space.

Photons, which are the carriers of the electromagnetic force, come in several varieties, classified according to their wavelengths which determine their energy levels. The varieties of photons listed in decreasing wavelengths and increasing energy include: radio waves, microwaves, infrared, visual light spectrum, ultraviolet, X-rays and gamma rays. Here on Earth, let us assume that each cubic meter of space holds the average of 400 million photons, only a fraction of which are of the wavelengths of the visual spectrum (our interest here) for which our eyes and brains have been constructed to see. We have good control over the number of photons that we need by automatically increasing or decreasing the diameter of our pupils, by opening or closing our eyes, by entering a well lit room or a room completely devoid of light, by recalling visual memories and by rapid eye movement.

The usual setting for sleep and dreams includes: a dark room, closed eyes, visual memories and rapid eye movements. The first two of these provide a dark background whereby the photons attached to visual memories, reinforced by those contributed by rapid eye movements, produce the bright, realistic images we experience in dreams.

Many of us have had the experience of the ringing of the alarm clock immediately becoming part of a dream or the pressure of a full bladder initiating a dream of desperately looking for a bathroom. These are examples of outside sensory stimuli (outside of the brain) being incorporated into dream content. Likewise, photons, released in REM sleep by deformation of the eyeball, are enough of an outside stimulus to be incorporated into dreams, lighting up their memories.

Light is the amorphous material of dreams. We have demonstrated in previously described experiments that deformation of the eyeball produces light directly proportional to the degree of deformation and its speed. The amount of photons released by the voluntary rapid eye movements alone, in the waking state with eyes closed, is unimpressive but definitely present. This causes us to wonder how many photons are necessary to light up the memories we experience in a dream.

When we see something, we immediately deposit it into our visual memory bank. It is not the memory alone that we deposit but also the photons that are intimately bonded to it. The less important or useless the memory is, the more rapidly it will decay. The vast majority of things that enter our memory banks through our eyes decay immediately, if they didn't we would be in big trouble; the storage capacity of memory is immense but it is limited, and so we must be selective as to what we want to store in memory and what we want to throw away with the garbage.

As previously stated, the massless photon is a cousin of the matterless memory. They travel together and cooperate and communicate well with one another. When we try to bring forth into consciousness a memory that is important to us, say, it is important because it gives a pleasant feeling, e.g., the memory of the Mona Lisa that Julianne recently saw in a museum (Figure 13), it is difficult to visualize it in our mind's eye with our eyes open. However, with our eyes closed, which we frequently do automatically when attempting a visual recall, it is "seen" with greater clarity. It is as if the photons of the present reality were in competition with the memory photons. From our experience we know that light appears brighter when viewed against a dark background. The billions of stars and other heavenly bodies disappear with sunrise and its attendant ambient light. The ambient light wins out. When we are asleep and dreaming, the memories become more lit up to the point where they appear as the present reality, not as memories of the past. How do we account for this astonishing clarity? Where do all those photons come from? They are "squeezed out" of the eyeball retina during the deformation that occurs with rapid eye movements. So, the photons incorporated in visual memories, serve us well, but alone they are insufficient in making a dream; more light must be added to make a dream feel real. The lack of competition from ambient light helps, but we need more photons to get that feeling of reality of being back in the museum, looking at the picture that has become such a pleasant part of our lives.

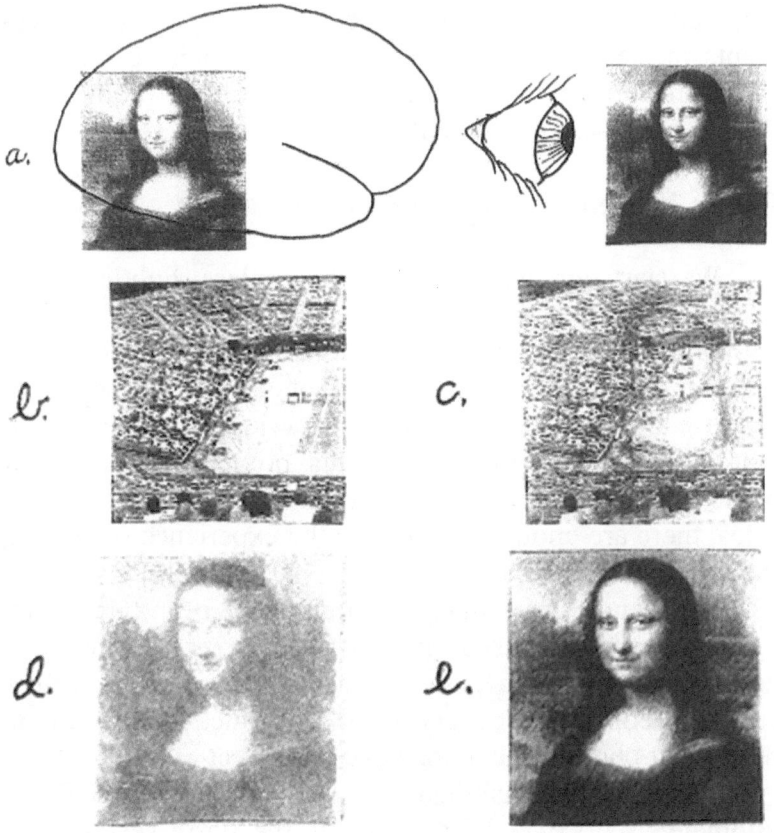

a. Julianne saw this famous painting while on a class trip to the museum.

b. The following day she watched this sporting event on television.

c. She recalled the pleasant museum experience, and the painting came to mind. The visual memory of the painting was obscured by the competing photons emanating from the TV screen.

d. Closing her eyes, the vision of the painting became significantly clearer, although ghostly.

e. That night she had a dream of the event, and envisioned a very clear image of the painting.

Apparently the photons released by the rapid eye movements in sleep reinforced the photons associated with the visual memory, filling in the missing pixels to produce the feeling of present reality that we experience in dreams.

Figure 13 Memory and Dream of Mona Lisa

We start our dreams with a photonless, lightless non-existence, without a correcting logical mind. In that kind of situation, together with the previously described chain reaction, not much in the way of photons is necessary to produce the realistic images we experience in dreams. So that even if rapid eye movements produce a paucity of photons, together with those incorporated in our visual memories, there are enough to produce the experience of turning the past into the present.

We wonder how many photons must be produced by rapid eye movements to put us into the dream mode; it doesn't take many. In 1942 Hecht, Shlaer and Pirenne, in a carefully constructed experiment, calculated the minimum number of photons the human eye can detect as nine.

Considering the singular speed of light (always 300,000 kilometers/sec.), which can encircle the Earth seven times within a second, and the relatively slow transmission speed of electrical impulses caused by photons in a neuron (100 meters/sec.) on their way to form images in the occipital lobe, only one photon in three million ever reaches that destination, and very many of those may not be of the visual spectrum variety and, consequently, invisible to the naked eye. So that even though we have access to billions of photons that enter our eyes, relatively few are useable in imaging. In spite of this, we see objects clearly enough in the waking state and just as clearly in our dreams. It surely is possible or even probable for just a few photons (maybe only one), released in REM sleep, to penetrate the storage vault of visual memories in the temporal lobes, causing the chain reaction that liberates enough visual memories to make a dream. Consequently, it is argued that REM sleep causes dreams and dreams do not cause REM sleep. In looking at the $D = mc^n$ equation, we should keep in mind that photons are a necessary component of *visual* memories. No photons, no visual memories and, of course, no visual dreams.

When an electron which is a negatively charged sub-atomic particle (matter) bumps into a positron which is a positively charged subatomic particle (anti-matter), they annihilate each other, and the annihilation results in the pro-duction of twin photons which, in this context, merit special names such as memoryton which is stored as visual memory in the temporal lobes and imageton which is stored in the vitreous or retina and, when released by rapid eye move-ments, together with memoryton forms the visual images of dreams. (The collision also produces an anti-neutrino which is of no interest to us here.)

The memoryton, acting alone, is inadequate in producing a dream image. It lives in the temporal lobe and is unable to get to the occipital visual cortex without help. In dreams, that help is forthcoming from the imageton, released from storage by rapid eye movements. These twins are reunited four or five times a night in the occipital lobe where all seeing is done.

The imageton that the memoryton was "born" with does not necessarily be the twin that helps transport brother memoryton into a dream. Since all photons are identical, any imageton can be the twin of any memoryton, and any memoryton can be the twin of any imageton, a statement that appears to be contradictory to the claim at the beginning of this chapter that there were several varieties of photons, classified according to wavelenghs. When we think of photons as waves we are aware of their multiple varieties, and when we think of them as particles we are aware of their exact sameness. In certain situations, to facilitate our under-standing, it is best to think of them as waves and in other situations as particles. There is no contradiction. Although I have been representing, for simplicity sake, the twins as a single pair, the reader should understand that they, most likely, have to exist as hundreds or thousands or millions of pairs in complicated dreams.

The fathers of quantum physics, Planck, Einstein, Bohr, Schrodinger, Heisenberg, de Broglie, Pauli, Dirac and others, great physicists all, were never able to come to an agreement on whether light was a wave or a particle since light has properties of both waves and particles, known as the *wave/particle duality.* In quantum mechanics, as opposed to classical physics, it would *not* be goofy to say that photons are flexible – they are waves when they *need* to be waves and particles when they *need* to be particles. I would guess that memorytons behave like waves because there is a certain vagueness about our visual memories that makes me think of waves. Imagetons, on the other hand, I think behave like particles because of the sharp, crisp borders of points of light.

Earlier this year, the physical community was overjoyed by the news that the Higgs particle (a.k.a. the God particle) and its field were proven to exist. That discovery helped to solve many problems in particle physics that physicists have been working on for decades. The Higgs field occupies every "nook and cranny" in the world we live in, even those between the nuclei of atoms and their orbiting electrons. Its job is to provide mass to all objects in our universe. We humans live in a Higgs field, and as a result, our lives and all of our experiences are with massive objects. Without mass we would be ghosts living in a ghostly world – massless bodies moving through massless doors. Mass is necessary for existence. We would not be without mass. Objects must be massive for us to feel them, to handle them, to work with them. We are not accustomed to any other way of living, even in dreams, except in a massive environment. In our dreams, to make them feel real as they do, it is necessary that those massless photons (which are also bosons) interact with Higgs bosons with their fields to give us that feeling of "being there". If the world we live in was deprived of that fundamental property of massiveness it would immediately be annihilated.

Let us assume that at some point when we are asleep, we have released an adequate number of photons that will allow us to form a clear image of, say, our-self sitting at a child's desk in the third grade classroom that we attended when we were ten. The image is quite clear. We may be amused by the absurdity of the scene. It's not a photograph; there is movement there, so it may be a video or a movie but it's not a dream unless we have that feeling of "being there", the feeling of being a *participant* observer. I believe that we get that feeling from the Higgs field because its omni-presence provides all objects in dreams with the same mass that we have become accustomed to living with in our waking life. To me, that feeling of "being there" is the most astounding property of dreams.

Looking at dreams through the eyes of a particle physicist, we might write a dream equation: **D = memoryton + imageton + Higgs field**

To make a long story short (if it's not too late), when we see a gorgeous woman, like limping Martha in Chapter 5, the memorytons and imagetons that she reflects into our eyes are stored in our temporal lobes and eyeballs respectively. We wish to retain her as a visual memory which, with help from rapid eye movements and the imagetons that they produce, enable us to see her in our dreams as a graceful, dancing ballerina.

In *A journey into Dreamland*, dreaming has been reduced to biology, neurochemistry, physics, quantum mechanics and, finally, to this *Twin Photon Theory of Dreaming*. Attempts at further reduction will force us out of quantum physics into the discipline of theology.

GLOSSARY

Abreaction The process of bringing to consciousness, and thus to adequate expression of memories, which have been unconscious because of repression.

Acetylcholine reuptake inhibitor A drug that prevents, by inhibition, the chemicals that cause the breakdown of acetylcholine, the important neurotransmitter involved in memory. Aricept is such a drug.

Adamization The author's neologism for the process by which a member of the hominid family becomes Homo sapiens.

Alchemy The empirical and speculative chemistry of the Middle Ages, concerned primarily with the transmutation of base metals into gold. Newton was an alchemist.

Analasandese The jargon used in social situations by those who are being psychoanalyzed.

Anthropic principle States that since humans are known to exist, the laws of physics must be such that life can exist. In its extreme form it states that the universe has been designed for man.

Archaea A domain of single-celled organisms that have no cell nucleus or any other organelles and are a separate domain in the three-domain system that includes archaea, eukarya and bacteria.

Anthropomorphic Having the outward appearance of a human being.

Autoscopy The psychological process in which the individual doubles his body image and projects it into the outside world; it is like seeing yourself in the mirror without the mirror. This frequently occurs in dreams.

Big crunch A model of the future of the universe in which it stops expanding and ultimately collapses on itself due to the force of gravity.

Big freeze A model of the future of the universe in which it will cool as it expands, eventually becoming too cold to sustain life.

Bonobo A hominid resembling a pygmy chimpanzee.

Castration anxiety Anxiety resulting from the anticipated loss of the male organ by castration because of the incestuous desire for one's mother as in the Oedipus complex.

Cerebral cortex The folded over surface of the cerebral hemispheres. It is the gray matter rich in layered neurons.

Circadian rhythm Pertaining to or designating those biological processes that tend to recur in cycles of approximately twenty four hours.

Clang associations When psychic associations are the result of sounds they are called clang associations. They are commonly observed in mania and schizophrenia.

Command hallucinations An hallucination, usually auditory, commanding an individual to perform a certain act, frequently suicide or homicide or self-mutilation.

Complexes A group of repressed ideas, interlinked in a complex whole, which besets the individual, impelling him to think, feel and act in a habitual pattern.

Corpuscular (particle) theory of light The theory that light is made up of particles as opposed to the wave theory of light.

Creationism The doctrine that the universe and all matter and forms of being within it are the result not of evolution but of God's direct and instantaneous creation.

Delayed memory A memory that, paradoxically, is forgotten immediately after an event but then is brought forth in close proximity to the event. It frequently occurs in relation to dreams.

Delirium A disorder of the sensorium in which orientation is impaired, the critical faculty is blunted or lost and thought content is irrelevant and incoherent.

Delusion A false belief without appropriate external stimulation and maintained in spite of incontrovertible proof.

Dementia Absence or reduction of intellectual faculties in consequence of known organic disease. Early on it is manifested mainly by defects in memory.

DNA (desoxyribonucleic acid) The chemical material of genes, packaged in our chromosomes, which transmits the instructions for building and maintaining our bodies.

Devolution Degeneration as opposed to evolution.

Dobsonian A type of large aperture, reflecting telescope, named after its inventor, John Dobson.

Dopamine A neurotransmitter important in schizophrenia and Parkinson's disease.

Ego That part of the psychic apparatus which is the mediator between the individual and reality. Its prime function is the perception of reality and adaptation to it.

Ego dystonic Anything that is unacceptable to the ego, e.g., an instinctual urge. Its opposite is ego syntonic.

Electra complex An analogue to the Oedipus complex, sometimes referred to as the female Oedipus complex. It is the unconscious desire of a daughter for an incestuous relationship with her father.

EEG (electroencephalogram) The graphic record of the electrical activity of the brain, usually obtained by means of electrodes attached to the scalp.

Electromyogram The graphic record of the electrical activity of muscle, usually obtained by the insertion of needle electrodes.

Entropy The measure of disorder of a system.

Epilepsy, temporal lobe A paroxysmal, transitory distur-bance in the electrical activity of the brain, arising in the temporal lobe causing a seizure. It is frequently accompanied by memory abnormalities.

Eukarya The domain of organisms whose cells contain a nucleus which contains genetic material.

Evolution The theory that all forms of life originated by descent, with gradual modification from earlier forms and so backward to the most rudimentary organisms such as bacteria.

Extra-ocular muscles The muscles outside of the eyeball but attached to it, that are responsible for the direction of gaze.

The Fall A biblical reference to the eviction of Adam and Eve from the Garden of Eden for disobeying God's command.

Free association The trends of thought or chains of ideas which spontaneously arise when restraints or censorship upon logical thinking are removed, and the individual orally reports everything that passes through his mind.

Galaxy An island of billions of stars, so named because of its milky appearance. Gk. Gala – milk. We live in the Milky Way galaxy.

Garden of Eden The biblical, utopian setting inhabited by Adam and Eve before "the Fall".

General theory of relativity Einstein's theory of gravitation that explains how the curvature of the fabric of spacetime causes the attraction of massive bodies.

Hallucination An apparent perception of an external object when no such object is present.

Hypnogogic hallucinations Hallucinations occurring prior to falling asleep.

Hypnopompic hallucinations Hallucinations occurring on waking from sleep.

Id The reservoir of psychic energy or libido that resides in the unconscious mind. It recognizes only its own needs. Its impulses may be modified by the ego and superego.

Illusion An erroneous perception of a sensory stimulus.

Imagetons The author's suggested name for photons that join with visual memories to produce dream images.

Inertial mass A body's resistance to acceleration.

Infantile sexuality The Freudian theory of psychosexual development which includes the oral, anal, oedipal and phallic stages.

Intelligent design The proposition that certain features of the universe are best explained by an intelligent cause, not an indirect or accidental process such as evolution.

Interpretation The formulation of the meaning or significance of a patient's verbal or non-verbal productions, and their translation into a form meaningful to the patient of his resistance, symbols and character defenses.

Manic state (mania) A mental state in which ideas are voluminous, feelings are intensely elevated together with marked psychomotor activity.

Medulla oblongata The lower brain stem responsible for autonomic functions such as pulse, blood pressure, temperature and respiration.

Memorytons The author's suggested name for photons that accompany deposited visual memories.

Mitochondria Organelles required for energy generation within the cell. They contain their own DNA and are thought to be bacteria that entered into a symbiotic relationship with man.

Natural selection The process whereby individual variations, advantageous to an organism in a certain environment, tend to become perpetuated in later generations. It accounts for "the survival of the fittest".

Newton's folly The author's characterization of Newton's experiment involving the incision of the tissue between the eyeball and the bony orbit.

Neurotransmitter A chemical released by a neuron at its synapse which has the effect of increasing or reducing the level of excitation in another cell, thereby increasing or decreasing the rate at which the second cell transmits signals.

Organelles The contents of the interior of our cells including the nucleus and mitochondria.

Oxidants Poisonous products of oxidation produced by mitochondria.

Parietal lobe The lobe of the brain that contains the somato-sensory cortex which receives sensory information about touch, temperature, pain and joint position and plays an important role in our appreciation of spatial relationships.

Parkinson's disease A neurological disorder caused by a decrease in the concentration of the neurotransmitter, dopamine, in the brain, resulting in tremor rigidity and slowness of movement.

PDR Physician Desk Reference is a book describing medications and their dosages, side effects and adverse reactions.

Peeping Tom A voyeur who experiences sexual pleasure from viewing the genitals of another.

Penis envy When the little girl finds out that the boy has a genital organ she does not possess, she begins to envy the boy and long for a penis.

Persistent vegetative state A pathological neurological condition in which only vegetative functions are apparent.

PET scan (positron emission tomography scan) A brain imaging technology whereby the metabolism of specific areas of the brain can be visualized.

Phallic symbol Anything that symbolizes the penis, e.g., knives, spears, guns, tools, trees, snakes, mice, birds, cars, cigars, pencils keys, telescopes, the number three, a variety of fruits, vegetables, hot dogs, sausages and many others. Designation as such is mainly but not entirely determined by shape.

Phocomelia A congenital malformation of development where the upper appendage of an arm or leg is absent so that the hands or feet are attached to the body like stumps. It is frequently caused by the sleeping medication, Thalidomide, taken during pregnancy.

Phosphene The scintillating concentric circles that are visualized when the eyeball is deformed by mechanical means.

Photon A quantum of light which is the mediator of the electric and magnetic forces. The photon has zero mass.

Photosynthesis The chemical process by which vegetation converts carbon dioxide and water into oxygen.

Pineal gland A cone shaped, rudimentary glandular structure found behind the third ventricle of the brain whose function is uncertain.

Pituitary gland A small rounded body at the base of the brain having a wide range of effects upon the growth, metabolism and other functions of the body.

Plathysmograph An instrument for recording variations in the size of various body parts, especially such variations as are caused by the circulation of the blood. It is frequently used in dream laboratories to determine changes in erectile organs.

Pons The part of the brainstem lying above the medulla that bridges the two cerebral hemispheres.

Proton The subatomic positively charged particle which, together with the neutron, forms the nucleus of the atom.

Protozoa Microorganism that are generally classified as unicellular.

Psychoanalysis A form of psychiatric treatment developed by Freud which investigates mental processes by means of free associations, dream interpretation and interpretation of resistance and transference.

Psychosomatic ailments Refers to a group of disorders whose etiology, at least in part, is believed to be related to emotional factors. At one time peptic ulcer was considered a psychosomatic ailment.

Quantum memories The author's designation of memories that appear to behave like quantum particles.

Quantum particles Subatomic particles of matter that frequently do not behave in the expected predictable fashion of classical physics.

Quark A truly fundamental particle in the atomic nucleus. The strong force arises from the interaction of quarks.

REM (rapid eye movements) The rapid to and fro movements of the eyes observed during that stage of sleep that is most often associated with dreaming.

Refraction The change in the direction of a light wave due to a change in its speed. This is most commonly observed when a light wave passes from one medium to another at an angle.

Relativity Includes Einstein's theories of general relativity which describes gravity as curvature in four dimensional spacetime and special relativity, based on the premise that the speed of light is the same for all observers regardless of their own motion. It also implies that the perception of time and space depends on the observer.

Repression The automatic unconscious process of keeping out, ejecting and banishing from consciousness ideas and impulses that are unacceptable.

Retina The inner layer of the eyeball consisting of cells, rods and cones which function in dim light and bright light and color respectively.

Schizophrenia A serious mental disorder characterized by delusions, hallucinations, disorganized speech, bizarre, disorganized or catatonic behavior, affective flattening and social and occupational dysfunction.

Steady state A largely discredited model of the universe in which the universe expands and new matter is created in the growing gaps between galaxies. The universe would thus remain in a similar density at all times and would last for eternity.

Srabismus The condition of being cross-eyed.

Temporal lobe The lowest lying lobe of the brain, above the ear, of special importance for memory, hearing, smell, language comprehension, visual recognition and emotion.

Third ventricle One of the fluid filled spaces at the center of the brain.

Thought experiment A type of experiment advocated by Albert Einstein in which logical thought is used to prove or disprove theories without the use of material laboratories.

Utility, primary, secondary and tertiary The various levels of usefulness of an object.

Visual electromagnetic spectrum The color spectrum visible to the naked eye including red, orange, yellow, green, blue and violet.

Vitreus body The transparent jelly-like tissue that fills the eyeball.

Voyeuristic tendencies The tendency to look at the genitals of another for sexual pleasure.

Wave theory of light A mechanism for the transmission of light energy in which a medium is not necessary for propagation. It is opposed to the corpuscular (particle) theory of light.

Wet dream A dream with sexual content in which the dreamer experiences orgasm with ejaculation.

INDEX

www.ingramcontent.com/pod-product-compliance
Lightning Source LLC
Chambersburg PA
CBHW020859310526
45786CB00018B/401